SIXTEEN

STUDY

STRATEGIES

SIXTEEN STUDY STRATEGIES

Innovative Notetaking System, Test Taking, Memorization, and More

JOHN L. TENNY, Ph.D.

Sixteen Study Strategies
Innovative Notetaking System, Test Taking, Memorization, and More

Published by **Learning Path Press**

ISBN: 978-8-9880537-9-8

Printed on demand by IngramSpark

First Edition 2020
First Printing 2020

10 9 8 7 6 5 4 3 2 1

For more information, contact:
learningpathpress@gmail.com

This book is dedicated to Dr. Leslie Carlton, who showed me how I learn and how to study. She changed my life. I also owe a debt of gratitude to the students who have used these strategies to improve their learning, the real goal of my efforts.

And I would never have gotten this finished had it not been for the encouragement of Grace Rubin and Glen Bledsoe. Their knowledge and insights have been invaluable and have resulted in a much more readable book.

Table of Contents

INTRODUCTION

Some students believe college is hard! The textbooks feel huge, and the print seems small. They find instructors go too fast, have too many assignments, and tests feel terrifying. These students discover there's not enough time between classes to get where you need to be, and it seems there's never enough time to finish the assignment before the due date. Whether you are preparing to start college or are where you know you need to do something if you're going to succeed, you have come to the right place.

Fortunately, you have a brain. And it's pre-programmed to learn. After all, you have already learned immeasurable amounts of information related to the world around you starting from when you were born. The task ahead is to focus this brain power by using specific strategies that have been designed to use the natural way the brain works for college level learning. When you apply the strategies in this book, you will learn, regardless of how difficult the subject.

Who Am I To Tell You How To Study?

I struggled through grade school with notes on my report card saying I was "lazy" and "works harder getting out of work than if he just did it." Flunked classes in high school and graduated in the lower tenth of my class. Went to college and flunked out in four quarters, even though I did the best I knew how. Not much of an academic record, right?

I left college, became a carpenter, got married, and moved on with my life. Then we had a daughter, and when she began school, I became interested in teaching. Although afraid I would repeat my past, I gave college another try and enrolled as a freshman at Illinois State University. In my first week as a returning student, I was directed to the Study Skills department and a wonderful, wise woman, Dr. Leslie Carlton. She worked with me on study skills, but, more important, taught me how I learn.

With that insight, I applied basic study skills and adapted other study skills to fit my learning style. Learning became easy almost immediately, and I went from a confused and worried student to a confident and highly successful student. As I continued to develop strategies for learning, college became a joy. After finishing my bachelor's degree in three years and graduating with Honors, I went on to complete a two-year master's degree in one year - the same person who flunked out ten years earlier.

I taught public school at the elementary and high school level for a few years, and then Willamette University in Salem, Oregon, hired me to teach part-time in the Education Department. Three years later, I began a doctoral program at the University of Oregon, graduating in 1988. Willamette University hired me full-time, and a year later, I was made Chair of the Education Department. Two years later, I led the team to create a new Willamette University Graduate School of Education, where I was the Director until retiring as Professor Emeritus. In 1996, Illinois State University inducted me into the Education Hall of Fame for my contributions to the field of education.

In a nutshell, the guy who barely made it out of high school and flunked out of college the first time, returned ten years later to graduate with Honors, complete a master's degree and doctorate degrees, and become the Director of a Graduate School of Education.

How could this be possible? What new skills helped me to succeed?

What Made The Difference

It was the set of study strategies I developed as a student and perfected as I taught College Study Skills for twenty years. These study strategies are based on how your brain works and have proven effective both for me and hundreds of other college students. Apply these strategies and find that learning is exciting and fun.

Instead of spending stressful hours reading and rereading, struggling to memorize and remember, and never being sure you can recall the information when you need it, you have a step-by-step system that engages your brain. You continually confirm that this knowledge is firmly in your brain and that you can access it whenever you want. And because this is all based on a natural way of learning, you find that it takes much less time, and you are confident and in control.

Even with all the embarrassment of the D and F grades, flunking out of college the first try, and the thought that I just might not have the ability, with these strategies, I quickly became a successful student. Getting A and B grades on quizzes and tests was an amazing and thrilling new experience throughout my bachelor's and master's degrees. And when, ten years later, I started on my doctorate degree, I wondered if these same tools would still work and at this level of learning. I dove into the coursework and found that it all was a repeat of my earlier success—top grades and a joy of learning. Success in learning breeds an excitement in learning that is the thrill of a lifetime.

When you use these strategies and activate your brain for learning, you have the tools to go as far as you'd like. While you might feel stress right now about getting good grades, when you find how easy and exciting learning is, you start setting your goals higher. Add these strategies to how you learn, and start thinking about the next degree. There is no reason to limit yourself—you have the drive and the tools. Think big!

Start now! Don't just read this book but apply the strategies as you come to them. Every single strategy you add to your set of learning tools moves you past the struggling amateur student. Do it NOW!

Read the important strategies 1 and 2, then dig into the KEYWORD Notetaking strategy 3. Pick a subject and take the KEYWORD notes before the next class. Do all the steps, and as you sit down in class, realize how ready your mind is to follow and understand the lecture.

As you listen to the lecture, note how active your mind is, how much you recall from the text, and how what the instructor says adds to your understanding. I clearly remember that first time when I realized that I really understood it all. It took my breath away! It's a great feeling to know that you have the topic firmly in your mind and that you have a strategy that really works.

What These Strategies Will Do For You

Less Time Spent Studying You spend less time studying because these study strategies are much more efficient than the typical efforts to learn. You might have to unlearn some habits you've picked up, but that won't be an issue. These strategies WORK and work immediately.

For example, did you know that you learn at the speed of electricity? When you process a new bit of information, your brain creates a new connection between neurons, and traveling down the nerve as an electric current, causes that neuron to connect to other neurons. This is learning taking place. This process occurs in everyone's brain and you will strengthen those nerve cell connections so that the electricity travels even faster. The result is quick and accurate learning and recall.

In addition, using these strategies, you improve your ability to read at the speed of light. That's right - your ability - since you already do that now. When you focus your eyes on words on the page, the image is transmitted to your brain at the speed of light. The note-taking and test-taking strategies will strengthen your ability to connect, store the images, and combine them with your current knowledge (you know a lot more than you think you do). And, just as important, these study strategies improve your recall of both the new and old knowledge when you need them. Like on a test.

Learn More One more thing: when you set up your brain through these study strategies to bring in the new knowledge, you learn while you sleep. Your mind rehearses and reviews the new knowledge, connecting it to what you already know, and strengthens those connections to make recall quicker and more accurate. It seems strange to say, but when you approach learning correctly, you know more when you wake up than you did the night before.

Strategies For Learning, Recalling and Test Taking

There are multiple strategies in this book: they are strategies for learning, recalling, and confirming that you have learned what you need to know, how to memorize and have it stick, how to take tests using the way your brain works, how to research and write papers, and more. A major error that even serious students make is to spend most of their efforts learning (the input) and minimal time on efforts to retrieve the information (the output), because they don't know how.

The study strategies presented here work together to engage your brain in an effective learning process. Instead of working much too hard on the input side, you discover that you learn things quickly and find the weak links in your recall. The whole process is quick and easy, and you have dependable confirmation that you both know and can recall the new knowledge.

Even better, you integrate the new knowledge into your whole knowledge system, strengthening both short- and long-term memory. Learning at its very best.

HOW IT ALL WORKS

Brain Based Learning

These study strategies are based on how your mind works. Since this isn't a biology course, there is no need to get into parts of the brain and what their functions are. However, here are a few things to help you understand why these strategies help you become a successful student.

Gestalt Functioning of Your Mind Gestalt psychology is a school of thought that looks at the human mind and behavior as a whole. Your mind works to understand new information and integrate it into your prior knowledge system by searching for any connections between new and prior knowledge - the dictionary defines Gestalt as "an organized whole that is perceived as more than the sum of its parts." You cannot stop your mind from struggling to find meaning. You can use that natural functioning of your mind to read faster, activate your brain to learn quickly, and to recall complex knowledge at will.

For instance, when you come across a new fact, your brain searches for any related prior knowledge and in that process, builds physical connections in your brain from any prior knowledge to the new information. If it doesn't find any, it creates a new storage point, and subsequent knowledge connects to this new point. As you access this stored knowledge or related new information, electrical impulses travel down the recall path. Each time this happens, it physically increases the size of that pathway in your brain. The result is quicker and more reliable access to information that you have retrieved multiple times. Many of these strategies are built on the Gestalt functioning of your brain.

Your PreConscious Mind All this occurs in your pre-conscious mind, which is active continuously, even while you sleep. Preconscious is that part of your mind that is just below your conscious thoughts. It's very active at processing new information and connecting it to your existing knowledge, day or night. As you apply these strategies, you learn to access and exercise the preconscious mind and improve learning, problem-solving, and instant recall. As you take in new information, it's helpful to give your pre-conscious mind time to process and solidify the connections between the new and prior knowledge. I call this Gestalt Time, and it, too, is embedded in these strategies.

Memory—From Short to Long You have a short-term memory and a long-term memory. Long-term memory enables you to recall information even though you haven't thought about it for some time. Short-term memories are things we need to know for the moment but not continually hold in our conscious mind. You can hold five to eight items in short-term memory. Any more items than that will quickly fade away, unless you rehearse or repeat them. The skill of a good student is to move things from short-term memory into long-term memory, and strengthen the recall path to the information, so needed facts come easily and quickly.

Go Professional Rather than stumble along as an amateur, be successful and adopt the attitude of being a professional student. Professionals take every opportunity to improve their skills, no matter how insignificant the effort may seem. It might include asking a question, using five minutes when the class is over early to double-check in-class notes, or quickly reviewing notes or vocabulary at the start of a class.

Imagine an amateur student walking into a classroom to take a test and thinking, "I hope I know this stuff." The professional is sure they are prepared because they have taken all the steps and used all the strategies here. They know that they know the material. That confidant attitude alone - "I am ready for this!" - increases your performance on the exam. These strategies are the tools to move you into being a professional student where you know exactly what to do to be successful.

Take the first step! Commit to implementing these strategies and trusting that your effort will pay off. Fortunately, the improvement in your learning is nearly immediate. Follow the steps in the KEYWORD Notetaking strategy and see a dramatic difference in the next class you attend. It feels like magic, but it is just using and engaging your brain in its natural way to empower learning and recall. Apply the Writing a Research Paper strategy and your preconscious mind does much of the creating and organizing while you sleep. Try the Speed Read a Novel strategy, and spend less time reading and still know more about the novel. The other strategies add additional skills, building you into a professional student.

Learn How You Learn It is important that you take control of your learning. Learning is an individual activity, and each of us is different. Finding out exactly how you learn best and what your particular strengths are help you adapt to any learning situation. If you approach learning in a way that is not natural to you, learning is more difficult and takes a lot more work. When you understand your own style of learning and apply that to the task, learning becomes easy, no matter what the task.

Here are some resources to give you some insights into different styles of learning. Dig into these and be on your way to being a professional learner.

Go to this site for different perspectives regarding learning styles. Different thinkers have provided a variety of ways to think about how you learn. Learning how you learn is an important step in taking charge of your life as a student.

https://www.mindtools.com/mnemlsty.html

Here is a site where you can take a Learning Styles Inventory. It's one model of learning styles, and a good place to start.

https://www.learning-styles-online.com/inventory/

Learning is easy. You do it constantly, whether it's how to make a pizza, the words to a new song, or how to add features to your phone. Academic learning is just another area, but one with built in time pressures, external evaluation, and new content that is not self-selected. Save time and stress by adopting strategies designed specifically to meet these learning demands.

STRATEGY 1

Do It Now!

> Decide to use these strategies
> Commit to gaining professional student skills

Because

> You are more successful with a focused drive and
> determination
> The intent to learn is key to success

It's Your Decision

The first thing you need to do is to commit to being a serious, focused student. As powerful as these strategies are, if you are just looking for shortcuts, you won't reach the level you need to be a successful learner. This is the time to look at yourself in the mirror and put becoming a skilled and dedicated student at the top of your list.

Being smart isn't the same as being skilled. A person can be intelligent but not skilled at being a carpenter, surgeon, or artist. Improving your skills at studying is a good use of your intelligence.

Make The Commitment

Commit to using the strategies that follow to improve your learning skills in both large and small ways. You may need to abandon old ways of doing things, things that may have worked fine in high school but are not beneficial in college. As you practice applying the strategies, do it with determination to become a powerful and successful learner. Go beyond just getting good grades and focus on becoming an educated person.

The amateur student goes to class, copies down notes on the board, listens to the instructor, and hopes something sticks. That's the passive approach, without the drive and determination that will make you into a highly successful student, both in terms of high grades and gaining new knowledge. It's exciting to realize that, with the right approaches, learning is easy, quick, and exciting.

STRATEGY 2

Do It Now !

Make a schedule
Tell your friends you are studying
Post a sign "Studying"
Use the small bits of time

Because

When you commit to focus your time on studying at every opportunity, you get more accomplished efficiently. The result is better preparation for class, increased learning and retention, and full control over your educational growth.

Learning First

The first commitment is to use your time to the best advantage. That starts with the determination to put learning first, right next to eating and sleeping. It's not that you shouldn't relax and have fun, and explore new interests beyond the classroom, but that studying comes before the distractions to your main goal.

Make a schedule that includes classes, study time, meals, necessary chores like laundry and shopping, and time to relax and have fun. Pay attention to travel times and locations. Amend the schedule to reflect reality if it takes more travel time than you thought, or you take longer to eat lunch while you chat with friends. And stick to it!

Announce Your Determination To Learn

A valuable technique for sticking to a schedule is to tell others when you are going to study. It sets the commitment in your mind and your friends will reinforce your efforts. By announcing to others that you are a committed student, they treat you that way, and they decrease the offering of distracting options.

Whether you live at home or in a dorm, or study somewhere on campus, make a sign "Studying. Do Not

Disturb!" Post it, and if someone interrupts you, politely but firmly ask them to come back later.

Use Every Minute

Use the small bits of time that are distributed throughout your day. The ten minutes that are freed up when the class ends early, the empty hour between classes, a few minutes after lunch that might have been spent checking Facebook are best spent taking textbook notes or reviewing the list of vocabulary words. Those small minutes effectively reinforce learning and accumulate an amazing amount of profitable time. When you use those time slots, you put learning ahead of leisure time and focus on applying study strategies. Because the study strategies are designed to be productive even in small bursts, you find yourself a successful, professional learner.

STRATEGY 3

Do It Now !

Take notes from the textbook before the class
Read and take abbreviated notes in a systematic way
Take in-class notes in line with the textbook notes
Review notes by expanding the abbreviated keyword notes

Because

Get ahead of your instructor so you have a general understanding of what they present in class. Taking abbreviated KeyWord notes causes your mind to process the text, and expanding the abbreviations practices and tests recall. Take in-class notes parallel to textbook notes, so it's all in the same outline.

> KEYWORD Notetaking is THE most important tool in your study strategies. This strategy builds your ability to store, retrieve, and connect old and new information, and increases your ability to listen to your preconscious mind. This strategy provides you with real power that benefits you not only as a student but also for problem-solving for the rest of your life.

Before you start

Get ahead of the instructor To make learning easy, it is important to get ahead of the instructor: set up your brain with a structure of knowledge by taking notes from your paper or online textbook before the class where the content will be covered. In most cases, a syllabus or an announcement in class will inform you about the next class content. If not, approach the instructor and let them know that you'd like to prepare before the lecture. This will mark you as a serious student.

Keyword Notetaking The amateur student is one who starts at the beginning of the chapter and plows their way, page by page, word by word, through the text. This typical process makes it harder to understand and retain the information - the result is a lower level of initial learning and a steep forgetting curve. Repeated reviews whenever there is time are just rereading with minimal gain, often followed by a cram session before the test. The diligent amateur can still only hope they know the content. With the KEYWORD Notetaking strategy, you know that you know!

In the KEYWORD Notetaking strategy, you go through the same material multiple times, each time with a different purpose. You build a structure of knowledge in your brain with, first, a broad overview, and then an increasing depth of information. And best of all, the strategy takes you less time than the read-and-reread amateur approach.

Let's start with some basics. First, never highlight or underline in your textbook. That is just identifying what seems to be important with an inferred intent to go back and learn it later - a waste of your good time. Get the details into your brain and then confirm that you can retrieve them at will.

Second, don't skip any step in the strategy. You make it harder on yourself if you take shortcuts. They are not there as a filler but are specifically designed to build retrievable knowledge.

Third, take every opportunity to complete another step in the strategy. The system is designed so you need not sit down and study for long periods. In fact, because of the KEYWORD Notetaking design, you make real progress in as little as ten or fifteen minutes of focused time. The time between study bursts strengthens your learning and recall.

The strength of KEYWORD Notetaking is that it automatically sets up puzzles in your brain. Your mind can't help but be engaged in resolving those puzzles while building a knowledge structure, providing built-in recall practice, and a system of confirming your learning. That's the Gestalt at work.

Analyze the textbook At the beginning of the term, begin by analyzing the textbook as a whole, how the topics are divided, and finding terms that are a mix of familiar and unknown. Parts of the text provide important information about the author's thinking and values, as well as parts that are only fluff and interfere with your learning. When checking out the textbook, you can zero in on what's essential, and view the topic as a whole. This is the first step in setting up the puzzle and activating your pre-conscious. You should not take any written notes yet.

Table of Contents Take a concentrated look at the Table of Contents. You don't need to do deep thinking here - but take a quick look at what this text covers, how it's broken into sections and subsections, and how new or unfamiliar it all is. Mentally note any parts that bring up something you've previously read or heard about.

Index—Key to Important Concepts Next go to the index, if there is one. The index is more than a list of terms and page numbers. It is a road map to the important concepts throughout the textbook. As you skim over this list of words, notice which terms have the most page references, showing these are likely keys to important concepts. Notice terms that are familiar (accessing your prior knowledge) and some you can barely pronounce (setting up the puzzle). Because of how your brain works, your preconscious will go to work to establish connections between the terms you focus on.

Graphics that add information - or distract Go back to the beginning and just flip through the text looking for any graphics, sidebar text, or cartoons. Some texts do a good job of providing graphics that add to the text information and this can be helpful to increase your understanding. However, many graphics, most sidebar text, and all cartoons are there to help the amateur student maintain attention to the textbook.

For you, as a professional student, these are often unnecessary distractions. An important attribute of a textbook is how font size, color, and bold text are used to show the outline of the content. Basically, you are getting an overall impression of a specific book and how the content is set up.

Notebook Layout Get a spiral notebook for each class. This is more important than you might think. The goal is to enhance your focus on each subject as you engage with it, whether studying or taking notes in class. Having multiple subjects in the same notebook makes it easier to get distracted. When you pick up the notebook for a specific course, you signal your brain to bring your related knowledge and experiences to the surface and be ready to receive new information.

Paper or Computer Its been found that paper-based notes result in longer retention of details over notes taken with a computer or tablet. The act of handwriting has a reinforcing impact on the information being recorded. Writing larger and leaving an extra space between lines makes it easier to reread and review your notes. Paper is cheap - don't make studying more difficult to save pennies.

Right side/left side It is very important to get ahead of the instructor, as this creates a structure for understanding new knowledge and incorporating it into your own knowledge system. You take notes from the text before the lecture, and you should set up the notebook to allow easy coordination of both pre-lecture and in-class notes. For right-handed people, take the textbook notes on the left page and in-class notes on the right page. In this way, you can take in-class notes aligned with the textbook notes and have an unobstructed view of both. Your arm won't be covering your text notes while you write the in-class notes. If you are left-handed, just reverse the layout. Do NOT take the text and in-class notes separately. It's important that they be together for efficient review and self-testing.

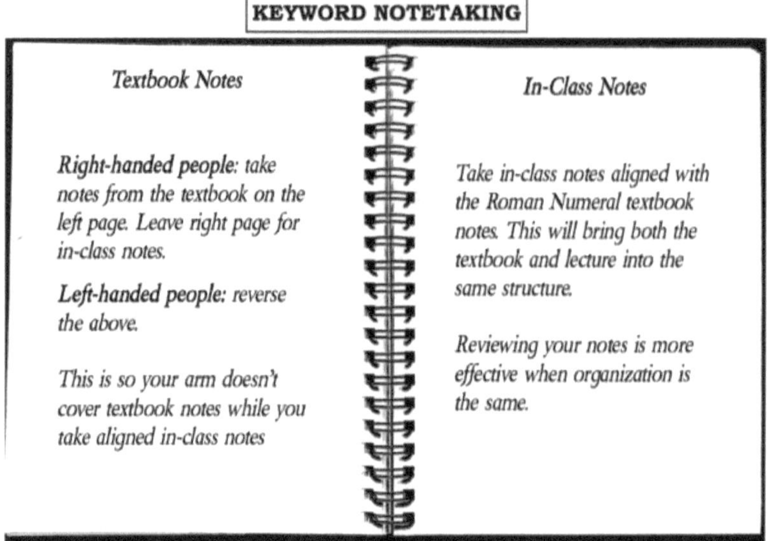

NoteTaking Your Text and Lecture

The KEYWORD Notetaking system differs from the traditional notetaking that tries to identify and condense important key concepts and details during the lecture while trying to remember what was read in the text. The KEYWORD system causes you to read actively and process the organized printed textbook information while setting up a system for self-testing your ability to recall the stored information.

The amateur student does little to practice what they need on a test - recall - by rereading their notes and going (again) through the chapter in the textbook. They are repeating the input stage of learning with minimal activity at the output stage, recall.

The KEYWORD system does both: first, by setting up a structured understanding of the topic, while creating a tool for practicing the critical recall stage. This system then integrates the information presented in a lecture with the textbook material and brings both into one clear, organized whole. Your set of notes provides ongoing recall practice and confirms that the information is actually within the learner's mind. Knowing that you know raises confidence and solidifies learning.

Importance Of Abbreviating Your Notes

Everything you write in your textbook notes should be heavily abbreviated, almost like a secret code that can include both text or symbols. Someone not familiar with the topic should have difficulty deciphering your notes.

Then, you create an abbreviation after reading a section of the text, you mentally manipulate that concept, and the active mental engagement builds a connection in your brain. And every time you look at that abbreviation and translate it into your full understanding, you have retraced the path to your stored knowledge and strengthened your ability to recall that concept at will.

Abbreviated Notes Example Below are the main headings from an Earth Science textbook with possible abbreviations. When you read the heading and create your own abbreviations, you are processing the text and creating a key to the stored information. If you can look at your abbreviation and translate it back to the full heading, you have confirmed that it's stored in your memory.

Textbook Headings	Abbreviations
I. World of Earth Science	Wld E Sci
II. Maps as Models of Earth	Mp Mod E
III. Mineral of the Earth's Crust	Min E Cst
IV. Rocks: mineral Mixtures	Rk: Min Mix
V. Energy Resources	Eng Res
VI. The Rock and Fossil Record	Rk & Fos Rec
VII. Plate Tectonics	Plt Tect
VIII. Earthquakes	Eq
IX. Volcanoes	Vol

If you find you can't immediately recall the information when translating your abbreviation, you have identified a "weak link" in your understanding. You now know exactly where to go in the textbook to reinforce that recall path.

Step One: Survey the chapter

This is a five-minute walk through the chapter without notetaking to get a feel for the task ahead. How long is the chapter? What are the bold-print clues to the structure of the chapter? Take a quick look at any graphics, maps, and pictures. You may not understand them and should not take the time now to study them — just set up the puzzle for your brain to work on.

If there are cartoons, read them. They will almost never be a source of related information and are actually a distraction. Get them out of the way before you start to take notes.

If there is a summary at the end of the chapter, read it carefully. This reveals the core information and helps you consolidate the details in the chapter. Some texts also include an important vocabulary list, and it is useful to read this carefully, even if there are no definitions included. Some terms will be familiar and some not, but all of them will set up the puzzle for your brain. This take only 5 minutes.

Step Two: Create a Roman Numeral Outline

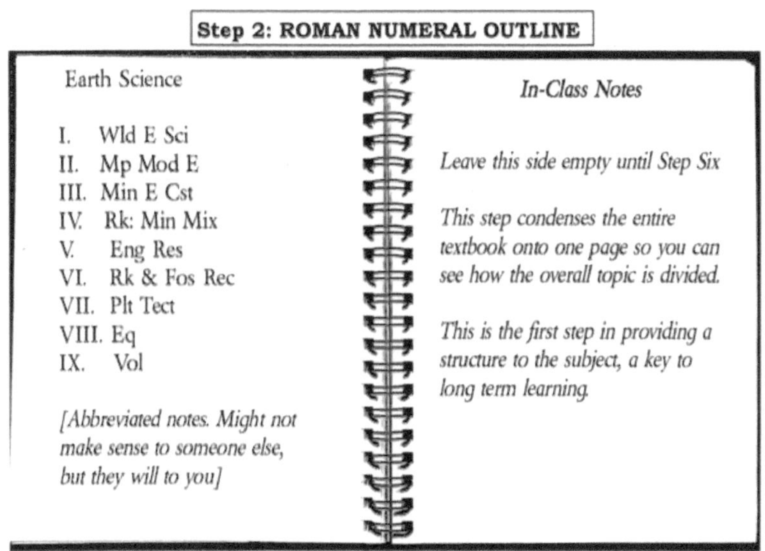

This is the first notetaking activity and serves to condense the entire chapter into a single Roman numeral outline on one page. This provides a holistic picture of the topic, and takes five minutes or less.

On the Textbook Notes side of your spiral notebook, abbreviate the title of the chapter and quickly look for the first bold heading. Abbreviate it and enter as Roman numeral I. <u>Don't read the text,</u> but flip pages until you find the next bold heading. Enter it right under the previous entry as Roman numeral II. Continue through the chapter, entering the abbreviated headings. Usually this fills about one page.

You quickly pulled all the main concepts together, mentally interacted with the terms. This sets your brain to searching your prior knowledge for anything related to these terms by trying to figure how any new concepts might be related. You have set up the structure for upcoming details to fit into, and activated your brain by setting up the puzzle.

Before you go to the next step, read and translate your abbreviations, best by saying them aloud. This only takes seconds, you have completed your first recall test, and strengthened your ability to recall this new knowledge in the process. If you can't translate your abbreviation, flip to that heading in the text to reinforce the term. Do not write out the full term.

Step Three: Read to take KEYWORD notes

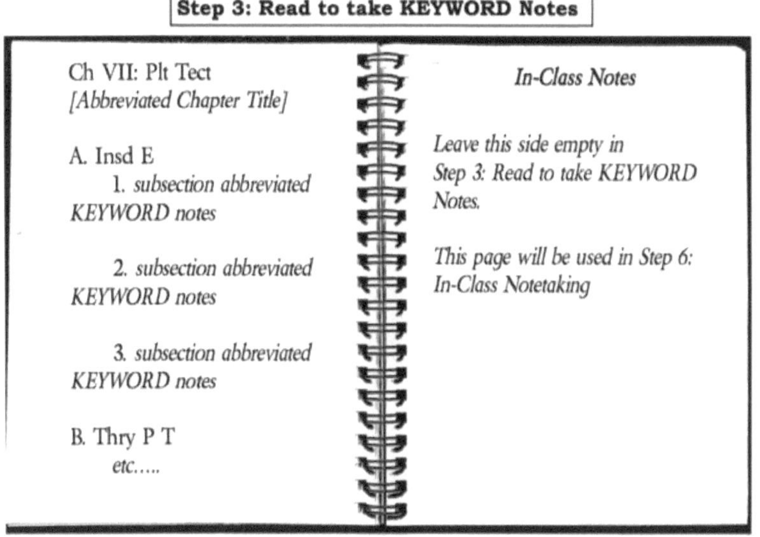

You condensed the complete chapter by abbreviating your top-level Roman Numeral heading, and then by translating the abbreviations, you strengthen your recall. This next step takes you deeper as you read the text paragraph by paragraph and take abbreviated KEYWORD notes, building and strengthening your recall path to the detailed content of the text. KEYWORD notes are a keyword or short phrase that, when you review it, brings back the full concept. Do NOT write out complete ideas or facts, but always abbreviate. That's the key to building and testing recall.

In your notes, write the abbreviation for the Roman Number I. Read the first paragraph or two until you identify the important concept or detail. In your notes, using an A, B, C, 1, 2, 3 outline style, reduce that concept or detail to a keyword or short phrase, and write an abbreviation for it. Work your way through the chapter, adding to the outline and recording each important concept/key detail in abbreviated form. Do NOT write out a complete word, phrase, or sentence, but ALWAYS abbreviate to create the KEYWORDS. You should be able to look at the KEYWORD and recall the concept or important detail.

There is a special benefit in this system: because it's a structured process, you can stop at any point if you run out of time or energy. If you stop mid-chapter, be sure to do Step Four: KEYWORD Review before you quit. This is a very important step in the KEYWORD NoteTaking system, needed to test your knowledge and strengthen recall. This only takes two minutes. Later, you can translate your existing KEYWORDS, then continue reading and taking your KEYWORD notes until you finish the chapter.

Step Four: KEYWORD review

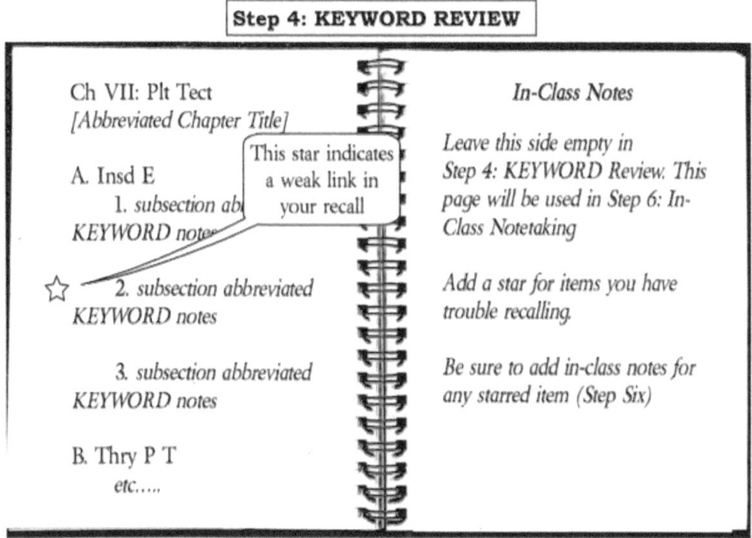

Whether you have completed the entire chapter, or just a section or two, it's important to realize what you have accomplished. You have read and interacted with the text in a structured manner, stored the knowledge in your brain, and created a system to test your recall. If you can look at your KEYWORD abbreviations and recall the concept or detail, you have confirmed that you have stored all that information in your brain.

Besides practicing recall, you also identify the weak links in your stored knowledge by easily identifying those abbreviations/keywords that you have difficulty translating.

Whenever you find a KEYWORD that you can't translate, simply go back to that spot in the text and review the concept. In your KEYWORD notes, put a star in the margin by each of those weak links — that alone increases focus on those items and strengthens recall.

Take a break. If you've taken notes on the full chapter or just a part, now is the time for a break, whether it's to go to another class, take a nap, or go dancing. During the break, your mind consolidates what you read and processed, and continues to connect it all to your prior knowledge.

Step Five: Get Ready Review

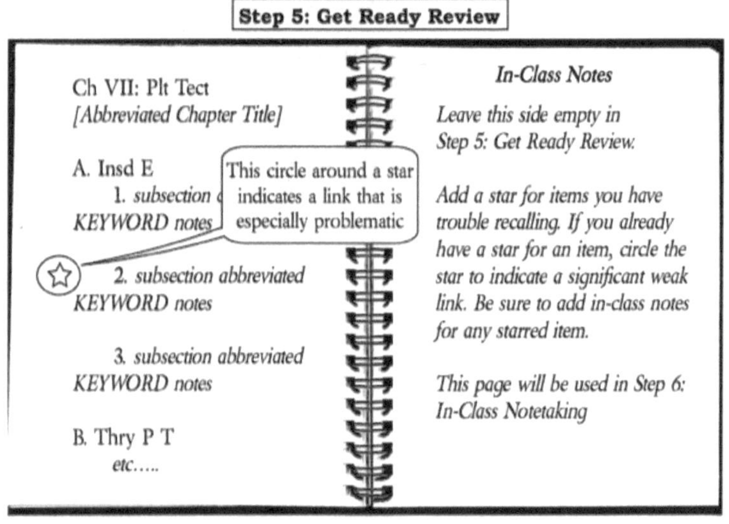

The Get Ready review is the step that brings your stored knowledge back to the conscious level after distractions interfere with accurate recall. Use this step when you return to a partially complete chapter to finish taking KEYWORD notes, or when you first go into the classroom. This only takes 2-3 minutes and is a very important step in solidifying your learning:

Open your notebook and mentally translate your KEYWORD notes, bring your stored knowledge to the surface and confirm that you really do have it stored in your mind and can retrieve it at will.

Pay particular attention to any item you starred in Step Four: KEYWORD review, as these were your weak recall links. If now you still can't translate the abbreviation, put a circle around the star to signal to yourself to review the text after the class, to ask a question during the lecture, or to change the abbreviation. Do NOT write out the full item - the abbreviation causes your brain to interact and work to recall the information.

Step Five is very easy and quick, best done right before the lecture starts so that the relevant stored knowledge is fresh in your mind as the instructor begins to talk.

Step Six: In Class notetaking

Take in-class notes on the right side of your notebook in line with the same topic in your textbook KEYWORD notes. If the instructor presents the information in a different order from the textbook, you are able to bring both into the same order by taking the classroom notes across from the Roman Numeral entry in your textbook KEYWORD notes.

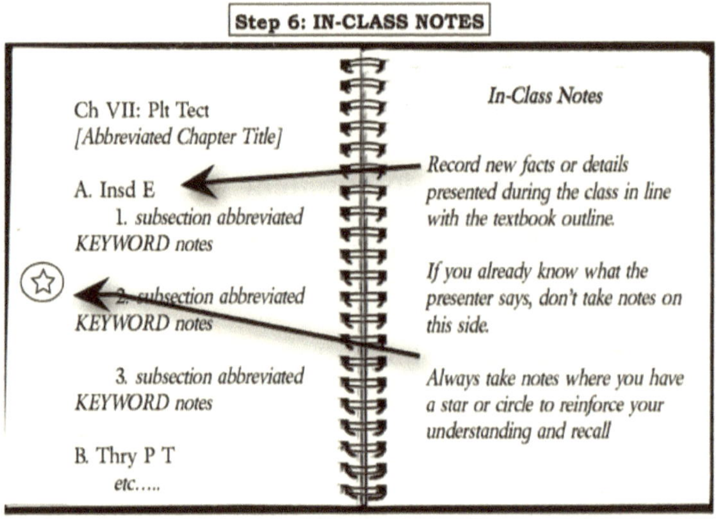

An important rule: don't take notes if you already know the information! That is, when you look at your KEYWORD abbreviation and mentally translate it, and you find that it's clear that the instructor is explaining something that you already know, is covered in the textbook, and included in your KEYWORD notes, so there is no need to write it again. It's actually in your mind and your ability to recall it from an abbreviation proves it. Focus on the new information.

The only exception is where you have put a star in your textbook notes. That's a weak link for you and can be reinforced by recording new, complete information from the lecture to add to what is in the textbook.

In this Step Six, don't abbreviate the notes you take. This is new information being added to what's in the textbook. You know that because you have the textbook outline to guide you. Developing your own method of condensed notes is fine, as long as you can easily read it later. Using this in-class notetaking step, you have more time to listen and think about what's being presented. Since your weak links alert you with the stars and circles, you are able to ask a timely, clarifying question. You mentally process the lecture material and incorporate it into the structured knowledge you already have stored and retrieved, and build a powerful understanding of the topic.

Step Seven: Put-It-All-Together review

The lecture is a linear process that you can't control as you take more detailed in-class notes. You may have jumped around in the textbook notes to align the instructor's presentation with those notes. This final Step Seven brings it all together as a comprehensive whole. Again, it's quick and easy, but very important for long-term learning and recall.

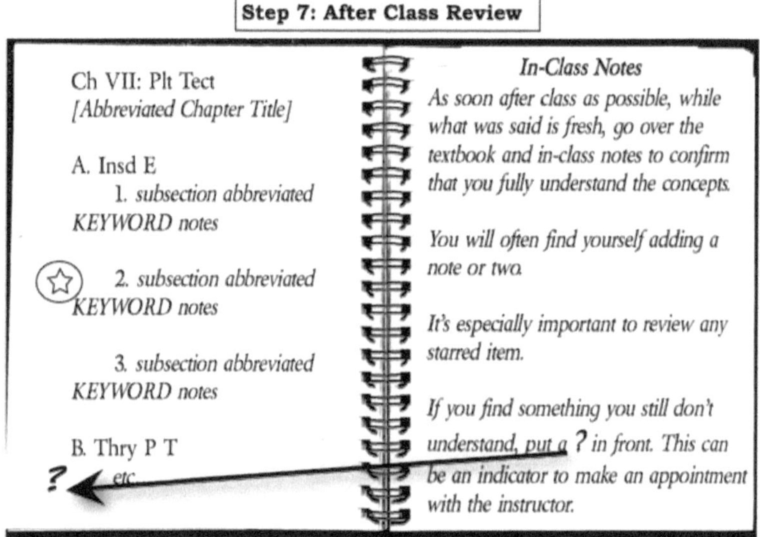

This Put-It-All-Together step is best done before you leave the classroom, while what is said during the class is fresh in your mind. The process is simple: just start at the beginning of your KEYWORD chapter and in-class notes to translate and recall both the text notes and what the instructor said just a few minutes before. If you wait an hour to do this step, you won't be able to remember exactly how the instructor said it.

During this final after-class step, you may add a short note to the in-class notes to clarify or reinforce some item. Because it's fresh in your mind, you are able to recall more accurately what the instructor said. If you find something is still confusing, you might catch the instructor before they leave the room. If not, you can meet and talk to the instructor, ask someone else in the class, or find another resource to help in your understanding. You know exactly where you have a weak link and can focus on reinforcing or gaining a better understanding.

Step Eight: New Chapter Review

When it's time to start on a new chapter, you start over at Step Three to take the KEYWORD notes from the text before the upcoming class. But before you begin the new chapter, take three minutes to go through the previous chapter KEYWORD and in-class notes to bring that knowledge to the surface of your mind. This facilitates connecting the upcoming new chapter and lecture to the previous knowledge and enhances recall.

STRATEGY 4

Do It Now !

Avoid taking linear notes in a live or recorded presentation

Use a graphic notetaking system

Ask questions if you don't understand

Review your notes immediately after the presentation

Because

The typical organized sequential notes work poorly in a presentation because a live speaker is more likely to talk in a less organized fashion. By using a flexible graphic notetaking system, you can convert a disorganized speaker into an organized structure. It's important to ask questions since there is no textbook to review. When the presenter leaves, your source of information leaves as well. Review your notes immediately so you can add additional notes while the presentation is fresh in your mind. If you wait, your recall will be less accurate.

When Traditional Notetaking Doesn't Work

Taking notes from a live or recorded speaker differs from textbook and lecture note-taking. Presenters at live events may not follow a clear outline, but often jump from point A to point B, back to point A, then on to point C. You can't use the KEYWORD notetaking system to get ahead of the presenter. If it's a presentation that you can't see or hear again, such as an in-person presenter, or a speaker on TV or radio, you cannot build an outline ahead of time. Even if you have recorded the presentation and can listen to it again, there is a common problem.

Unless the presenter is very organized and the presentation is pre-scripted, there is a tendency for live presenters to refer back to a point previously made and add new information. This jumping around by the presenter makes taking notes in the traditional Roman numeral outline difficult and ineffective.

From Disorganized Speaker To Organized Notes

Windmill Notetaking is a technique for recording notes in a way to bring the disorganized speaker into a single, clear outline — one that is clear and much easier to follow and review.

If you are at a live presentation, sit close to the speaker to reduce distractions and be able to hear what's being said. If you are listening to a recorded presentation, removing distractions, both visual and auditory, is equally important.

A hint: if you have a recorded presentation that you can rewind, go to the last ten minutes of the presentation, when speakers often summarize their talks and restate their main points.

Windmill Notetaking

The first graphic shows how to set up your notebook, and includes a central topic box and radiating lines for main points and details. There is also a Sidebar Page to record quotes, statistics, or important facts.

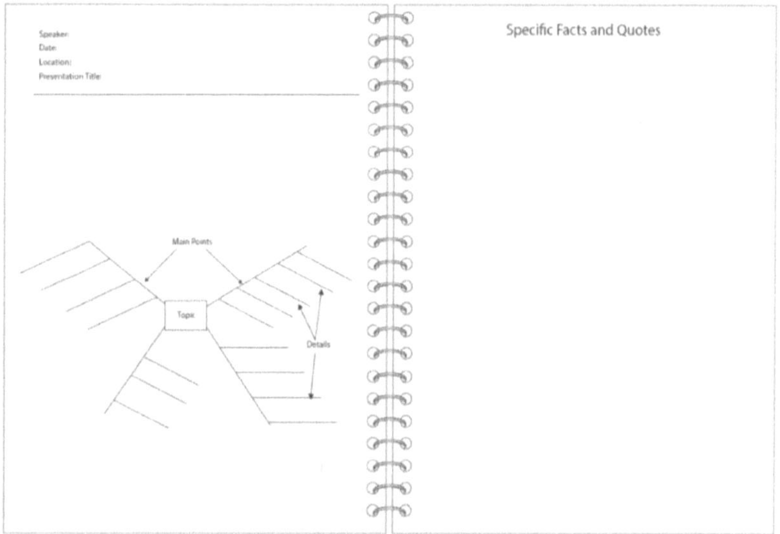

As you take notes, listen for main points, draw lines, and add notes. Once you record the main point, add lines and notes under that main point. Listen for references to a previous main point and go to that main point line to add to the details there. This Windmill Notetaking technique brings the random speaker into a clear outline system, an effective strategy.

In the center box, write the title of the presentation and draw a line from that box for each main idea, and label it. Many speakers reveal the main points in their introduction to the subject: "Today I will talk about…" If the speaker doesn't, add the main point lines as they occur, leaving room for detail lines and notes. The Sidebar Page on the opposite page is available to record specific notable facts.

In the example following, imagine the speaker starting out talking about KEYWORD Notetaking, but in the middle jumping to Multiple Choice Tests. You would just draw a second line, label it Multiple Choice Tests and take appropriate notes there. Then, when they return to the KEYWORD Notetaking topic you switch back to that line for further notes. No matter how the speaker wanders, you have an organized and coherent set of notes.

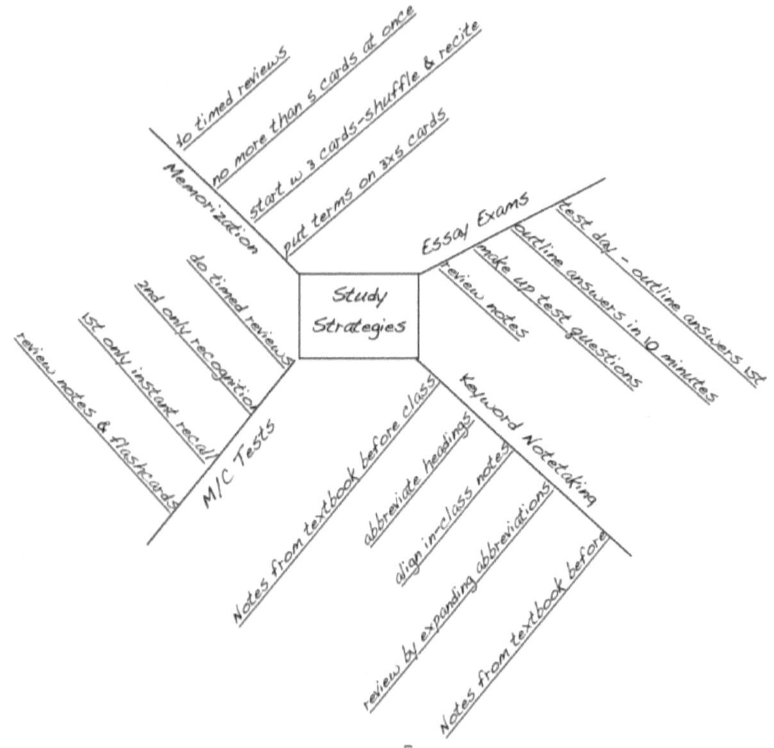

After The Presentation

Follow up to the presentation is very important. When you listen to a live speaker, it is a linear, one-time-through process, and you want to review your notes while they are fresh in your mind. You add notes to clarify or expand what you have written and take additional notes on the Sidebar Page to record your own thoughts or question and response to the topic. If a Roman numeral style outline is helpful when reviewing your notes, you can easily and quickly convert this graphic outline.

Pre-test Review

To strengthen your recall of the live video or audio presentation, do the follow-up review as soon as possible after the presentation for the most effective results. Go over your notes again after 24 hours to further enhance recall. Since you have coherent notes from this live or recorded presentation, you have an effective tool for the pre-test review.

A useful technique, both for self-testing your recall, as well as in the actual test, is to draw an empty windmill on a piece of notepaper and add the text, including what you wrote on the right page, without looking at your notes. Just having the blank windmill drawn in the margin during a test strengthens your recall.

JOHN L. TENNY, Ph.D.

STRATEGY 5

Do It Now !

Feet on the floor. Ready, Set, Go!
Skim through the text in a random pattern
Listen to your mind as it connects the random words
Output your thoughts by taking notes or speaking aloud

Because

When you read aggressively, pushing yourself, you find it easier to concentrate and engage your mind more actively. When you skip rather than reading word by word you activate the Gestalt of your conscious and pre-conscious mind, and an active mind increases learning. And as you skim the text, become aware of your mind as it races to connect the terms. When you aggressively read a section and then take notes, you move from input (reading) to output (notetaking), which strengthens your ability to remember and recall this new knowledge.

Reading is Thinking

I'm going to redefine reading for you. It's not looking at each word one by one to learn what the writer is saying. It's not a passive act, and definitely not just memorizing what's on the page or screen.

Reading is thinking and intertwining what you already know and have experienced with what the writer is saying. And you can read at the speed of light and process at the speed of electricity - that's how your brain works.

Speed of Light

The image of the words on a page is transferred to your brain when you focus on the text, and that happens at the speed of light. When you focus, even for an instant, your brain captures that image. Your brain then stores, sorts, and integrates that detail with everything else in your brain by sending electric charges along the neurons in your brain, at the speed of electricity. You read and assimilate information faster than you have ever realized. And it's not a new skill — it's what your brain already does. Your job is to get in touch with your brain—your pre-conscious—to retrieve the newly stored knowledge at will. That's called listening to your brain. It's also something you do all the time, and you confidently rely on that ability. The study strategies here build upon this under-used ability, accessing the power of your brain, and turn you into a powerful, skilled, and fast learner.

The basis of Aggressive Reading and learning at speeds beyond your wildest imagination is an attribute of your brain based on the Gestalt theory. Simply put, it's the drive of your brain to create whole images or understanding from the parts, which results in an understanding of the whole that is greater than the parts.

For example, when you see the words "book, tablespoon, ingredients," your brain searches all the stored knowledge that relates to those three words (and remember, it's at the speed of electricity) to close the "how are these three words related" gap. That is a puzzle your brain is trying to solve, and you can't stop it from happening. If you come up with the word "cookbook" as a connection, your brain brings to the surface of your consciousness everything you know about the words book, tablespoon, ingredients, and cookbook. If you add "loaf," your brain instantly re-sorts and reorganizes your quest for understanding to include bread, or meatloaf, or even sugarloaf, and also searches for confirmation of the correct connections.

Your Brain Fully Engaged

So, putting all this together, the speed with which words come into your brain, causing your brain to become fully and automatically engaged, not only makes learning easier, but also integrates new knowledge with old in a manner that enhances recall and long-term memory. The key is to read in such a way as to create the puzzles that cause your brain to strive to solve the puzzle. It's easy to do - and uses the power of your brain.

Look at the charts below. As you read the text, notice how your mind instantly works to create meaning from the vague parts. The more you read this way, the better you are able to bring your prior knowledge to bear on the "puzzle." As you use your brain's ability to instantly capture the text, your processing speed increases, and your skill in processing and integrating knowledge becomes more accurate and efficient. You are building the skills of a power learner.

Turn the page for an aggressive reading passage with key text visible and the other text hidden, illustrating how your eyes might skip through a text and see only random words or phrases. Your pre-conscious mind works to make meaning by pulling together prior knowledge about the topic and, using your logical mind, to determine what the passage is about.

Read the visible words as fast as you can. Then close your eyes and think about the passage, letting your pre-conscious mind bring understanding to the surface and into your conscious mind. Note any connections between the visible words that seem unclear.

AGGRESSIVE READING CHART ONE

Jesse Woodson James

                    outlaw

Missouri

Southern   Frank

James   guerrillas

        American Civil War

William Quantrill   "Bloody Bill" Anderson

                    atrocities

    Centralia Massacre in 1864

After the war

               robbed banks

                   popular sympathy

       most active

         until 1876

           bank

Minnesota several

captured   killed

       Jesse James   killed by

Robert Ford

Now turn the page for the full text. Was your understanding of the passage correct?

Are you wondering if you would land on important terms if you skipped around? Try this—vertically cover 3/4 or 2/3 of the text on the next page and read the remaining. Notice what your mind is doing as it works on the puzzle. Some parts you fill in because you already know about Jesse James; other parts you use logic and assumptions, but in either case, you actively involve your mind. That's the key to easy learning.

Truth is, you can't stop your mind from pulling together everything you know to make a prediction. That activation of your mind is powerful and increases as you repeat the practice.

AGGRESSIVE READING CHART TWO

Jesse Woodson James (September 5, 1847 - April 3, 1882) was an American outlaw, bank and train robber, guerrilla, and leader of the James–Younger Gang. Raised in the "Little Dixie" area of western Missouri, James and his family maintained Southern sympathies. He and his brother Frank James joined pro-Confederate guerrillas known as "bushwhackers" operating in Missouri and Kansas during the American Civil War. As followers of William Quantrill and "Bloody Bill" Anderson, they were accused of participating in atrocities against Union soldiers and civilian abolitionists, including the Centralia Massacre in 1864.

After the war, as members of various gangs of outlaws, Jesse and Frank robbed banks, stagecoaches, and trains across the Midwest, gaining national fame and often popular sympathy despite the brutality of their crimes. The James brothers were most active as members of their own gang from about 1866 until 1876, when as a result of their attempted robbery of a bank in Northfield, Minnesota, several members of the gang were captured or killed. They continued in crime for several years afterward, recruiting new members, but came under increasing pressure from law enforcement seeking to bring them to justice. On April 3, 1882, Jesse James was shot and killed by Robert Ford, a new recruit to the gang who hoped to collect a reward on James' head and a promised amnesty for his previous crimes.

Self-testing Activates Your Brain

The more you practice this skipping/skimming technique, followed by listening to your pre-conscious mind, the more accurate your understanding and recall become.

The Physical Part

As you move from being a passive reader to an aggressive reader, you also change how you physically read. When you read a novel for pleasure, it's fine to lie on the couch, have the TV on, and completely relax. That's NOT what you should do when studying, even if the assignment is to read a book.

Sit at a well-lit desk or table, feet on the floor, and push to read faster with greater focus and concentration. The more you concentrate on the task at hand, the fewer distractions draw you away. When you sit down to read, think "Ready, Set, GO!" and dive into reading and understanding as quickly as you can, even faster than you are comfortable doing. Your brain adjusts to the new speed, and you get better and faster at aggressive reading.

STRATEGY 6

Do It Now !

Set up a notebook to take notes as you read
Read beginning, middle, and end sections of the novel
Take breaks between reading each section
Read every fifth page in one sitting.
Use your notes for pre-exam review, paper writing, etc

Because

Taking notes as you read keeps you consciously focused on the novel. Reading separate sections activates the Gestalt functioning of your mind and creates the puzzles that engage your conscious and pre-conscious mind. Taking breaks between reading enables your pre-conscious mind to process and consolidate the story. The every-fifth-page strobe read enables you to see the flow of the novel and the development of the characters and conflicts. The notes will be very useful at a later date to bring the details back into your conscious mind.

Notetaking a Novel

The Goals Consider the goals of reading a novel assigned as a class project. The instructor would like to have you become actively involved in the novel as opposed to just a passive reading of the words. It is important that you know the who, what, when, and where of the actions presented. Noting the changes in the characters as the novel progresses and being aware of the conflicts and outcomes is critical to understanding the author's purpose and experiencing the novel as a whole. The Notetaking a Novel Strategy does all that and more.

Notebook Setup An important facet of this strategy is to take notes as you read. This process results in active involvement in a combination of input (reading) and output (taking notes). This strengthens your ability to follow the development of the novel and increase recall. Notetaking a Novel provides the additional benefit of a way to read at different times and when reviewing your notes, bring the details to the surface of your mind.

Set up a chart in your notebook. On the left page, create columns with headings of characters, description of the characters, a change in the characters, and outcome of the characters at the end of the novel.

Title, Author, Publisher, Date			
Character	Describe	Change	Outcome

On the right are three columns with headings of First Reading, Second Reading, and Third Reading. Under these headings are cells for Setting and Conflict. Under the Third Reading, Conflict becomes Outcome.

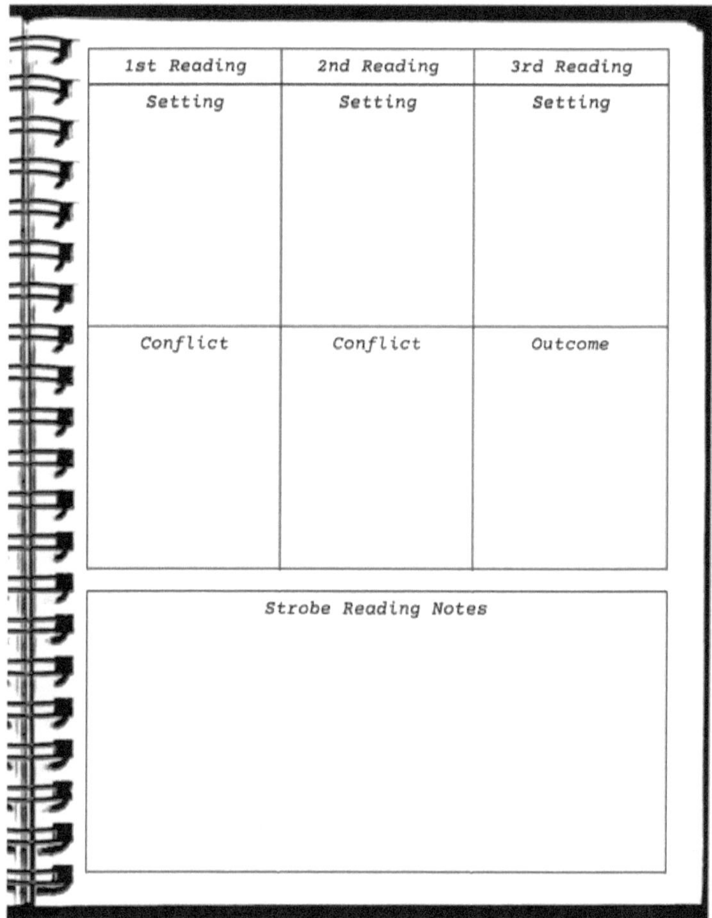

With both the novel and short story notebook layouts, add columns for any additional component that the teacher assigns, such as dialogue or flashbacks. This can be on the right page.

This strategy is to read the novel in four stages in a process that sets up a puzzle, resulting in mental engagement.

Step One: First Twenty-Five Pages

Read the first 25 pages or ten percent of the novel, whichever is greater. As you read, write each character's name in the Character Name column, and a short description of the character's role in the Character Description column. During this first reading, leave the Character Change and Character Final columns blank. In the First Reading column, note the setting and any conflicts that occur.

It's important to understand how different this process is from the typical way the amateur student reads an assigned novel. Usually it's a matter of leaving the novel reading until other studying is finished, dinner is over, and then plopping down on the couch to start the assignment. Often, the eyes begin to droop or a favorite TV program starts — and the page gets dog-eared. With the Notetaking a Novel strategy, you go through the first 25 pages, interactively taking notes and creating a record of what you've read. Like the amateur, you take a break, but you are prepared for the next step.

Take a Break It's important and useful to take a break, to give your pre-conscious mind an opportunity to process what you've read and to predict what might happen next. Take a walk, listen to music, eat lunch, or, if it's the end of your day, go to bed. Nothing you do stops your pre-conscious from processing this new information. When you return to do the second reading, review your notes to bring the details to the surface.

Step Two: Middle Of The Book

For the second reading, jump to approximately the middle of the novel and read 25 pages or ten percent, whichever is longer. As you read, record any changes in the characters from the first read and add any new characters and descriptions. Leave the Character Final column blank. Update the Setting and Conflict columns.

So, what do you know at this point? You have identified the main characters - the main characters always appear in both the beginning and middle of the novel. You know at least part of the minor characters - they come and go as needed to interact with the main characters. You have details about the changes in the setting and progress of the conflict and potential resolution. Your notes give you a device for reviewing what you've read as you write a report or prepare for a quiz.

Even more important and powerful is what you've set up in your brain. Because of the time passing between the first and second readings, you cannot avoid becoming mentally engaged with the novel. Your conscious and pre-conscious work to resolve any changes in characters, setting, or conflicts between the first and second read. This happens even when you're engaged in other activities.

Take a Break Again, take a break. This can be a short fifteen-minute cup of coffee or a full day of classes. When you return, read your notes and think about the changes between the first two readings — listen to your pre-conscious mind's solutions to the puzzles.

Example: In the first read, there is a man who is a banker, a doting father, and a respected member of the community, and a teenage, rebellious daughter who has just broken up with her boyfriend.

In the second read, the father has been fired and is despondent over his daughter's arrest and being put in jail.

Your mind cannot avoid searching for clues to explain the changes. Did the father embezzle money, or is he a secret, abusive drunk? Is the daughter innocent, or did she get involved with some bad people? Clues are given, and your mind processes lots of options. The key is that you are actively involved with thinking about the novel, much better than just a passive read, and hoping the details stick.

The amateur, passive reader reads a portion of the book, dog-ears it, and goes on to something else. They get comfortable on the couch after dinner and start reading where they left off. It takes several pages for them to catch up with who the characters are and what the novel is about. They have not taken any notes. They read for a while, dog-ear a page, and go off to do something more interesting.

Because of this stop-and-start approach, without notes, amateur learners find it difficult to become engaged in mentally processing the text. As a result, they achieve only a cursory understanding of the novel.

Step Three: Final Twenty-Five Pages

For the third reading, go to the end of the book and read the last 25 pages or ten percent, whichever is longer. In the Character Final column, record how the characters are doing at the end of the novel. Describe the final setting of the novel in the Setting box. In the Conflict Outcome box, write how the conflict is resolved.

Your mind races now. Both your conscious and pre-conscious minds use the clues in the final section of the read, in combination with the notes from the first and second read, to make sense of the entire novel. There are unresolved gaps that your mind will struggle with, and you continue to be actively engaged with the novel.

Example: In the last pages, you find that the father is back at the bank and has been promoted, the daughter is beginning her first year of college, and the town sheriff has been found guilty of extortion and attempted murder. How in the world did all that happen?

Take a Break Take the last break to mull over, conscious and pre-conscious, what you know about the novel, and let your mind fill in the gaps. If you go about your other activities, I guarantee you the story will repeatedly pop up in your mind as your pre-conscious tries to resolve the gaps in the story. You are actively processing the novel. Review all of your notes before the final strobe reading.

Step Four: Strobe Read

In the fourth reading, read the entire novel in one sitting, but with a twist. Start at the beginning and read every fifth page. Since you already know the major and minor characters, the changing setting, the conflicts, and how they are resolved, you can read much faster. Read to confirm or amend your thoughts about what happens during the unread pages. Look for character development, the flow of interaction between characters, and the style of writing.

This step is like watching a performance with a strobe light that goes on and off quickly, showing only part of the action. You don't see every detail, but you can witness the dancer's movement, and your mind completes the actions. As your mind processes the small gap between the first and fifth pages, it combines your prior knowledge and thoughts with the new clues in the Strobe Read, and pulls the story into a single flowing idea.

During the Strobe Read, take notes on the novel as a whole, on anything that surprises you, and any specific attributes of the writing as assigned by the instructor, such as dialogue, or how characters were introduced or described.

The notes don't have to be extensive since the story is firmly embedded in your memory.

Your Notes Keep It All Fresh

When you finish the Strobe Read step, review your notes again, and add any last-minute thoughts to solidify the novel in your conscious mind. As you go about your daily activities, other unrelated learning takes place that interferes with recalling the details in the novel, and that's why it's critical to have notes. You need to bring the novel into your conscious mind when it's test time, or you have a related writing assignment. Your notes do just that.

Notetaking a Short Story

The process of notetaking a short story is similar to notetaking a novel, with a few changes. Read the first, middle, and last ten percent of the story, use the same chart with characters, setting, and conflict headings to take notes, and take a break between reads. In the Strobe Read step, read every <u>third</u> page.

With both the novel and short story notebook layouts, add a column for any additional component that the teacher assigns, such as dialogue or flashbacks. You can always go back and read each page to focus on language use, character development, deeper meanings, etc. If you need to focus on more complex facets of the novel, it will be easier and faster since you already know the basic details of the novel.

A Very Advanced Tool

If you want to go deeper into understanding the structure of novels, there is a tool. It is appropriate for English majors or those interested in a career as a writer.

Fabula is a set of cards originally designed to aid authors in structuring and organizing an idea for a novel. The creator has done significant research using the tool to analyze existing novels and provides useful examples. The main set of cards guides the identification of characters, conflicts, plot points, resolution, and much more in an assigned novel. The result is an in-depth and detailed analysis of a novel, appropriate for the serious novel reader.

Go to the Fabula website, https://fabuladeck.com to view examples. The product comes as either a set of physical cards or as a download file for printing. There is also an informative video by the author at:

https://vimeo.com/355573964/7ff23972ab

Amateur versus Professional

Imagine the final assignment is to compare two novels worth sixty percent of the grade: the first and second novels assigned and discussed. Over two months since reading the first novel, and the task throws the amateur student into a panic. They barely remember the story and confuse the details with the other four novels read during the term. Their only option is to reread both novels and try to keep things straight — a time-consuming and stressful task.

But not you, the professional student. You pull out your notes from both novels and quickly bring the characters, plot, conflict, and resolution into your conscious mind. Comparing the components of the two novels is straightforward and stress free. You have time to complete this assignment, and to study for other upcoming exams. With your KEYWORD notes organized and efficient, you go into those exams with confidence - the mark of a professional student.

STRATEGY 7

Do It Now !

Put the terms on 3x5 cards
Start with three cards, Shuffle and recite
No more than five cards at a time
Do timed reviews

Because

Getting the terms on individual cards lets you separate those you have learned from unknown terms. Starting with three cards is within your short-term memory and shortens the time needed to learn the terms. Always shuffle the cards and mix them front and back to strengthen learning of the individual terms. Don't work with more than five cards at a time, one of which is a new term.

> This keeps the number of terms you are learning and reviewing within your short-term memory capacity. To move the terms into long-term memory, you must do a series of reviews in spaced amounts of time.

You Can't Memorize Your Way Through College

Trying to memorize your way through college does not work. That said, there are several typical assignments that require instant recall of isolated facts, such as vocabulary, dates, and locations, and formulas. Sometimes the exercise is even more complicated than a word and definition task, as in an Art Appreciation course. There, you need to identify the object (Jane Avril painting), the artist (Toulouse-Lautrec), and the period when created (1899), making memorization more difficult.

The Memorization Problems

There are two main problems with memorization of lists: they take a long time to reach 100%, and 48 hours later, you have forgotten 75% of the terms. Research studies on memorization show that without review, the rate of forgetting is very steep - over 50% within an hour.

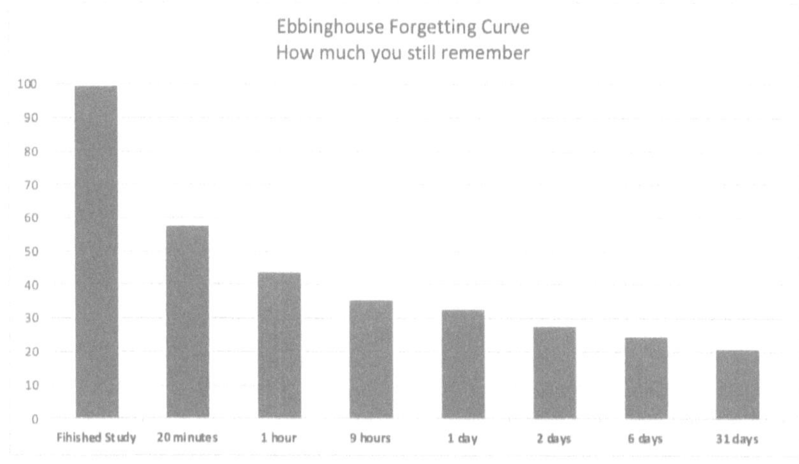

This is because your short-term memory can only hold 5 to 7 items at one time. You must move an item into long-term memory, or you will lose it. This memorization strategy shows how to decrease the time needed to reach the 100% memorized level and, through a systematic review, move the terms into long-term memory.

As an example, the assignment is to memorize 25 biology terms and definitions for next week's quiz. The diligent student starts out by putting each term on a 3 x 5 card with the term on one side and the definition on the other. This recommended first step because it enables you to manipulate the terms in ways that increase learning.

Amateur Student Mistakes   Amateur students make several mistakes at this point, resulting in a more difficult task than necessary. They begin by stacking the cards with the word face up. They work through the full stack of 25 cards, looking at each word and trying to recall the definition.

The problem is that they are memorizing the terms in a sequential order. In their recall efforts, the forgetting of one term can break the chain and make recalling the next term more difficult. In addition, by going through the full stack each time, they overload their short-term memory and increase the time it takes to reach a 100% memorized level. There is a better way.

The Better Way

Shuffle and recite Once you have all the terms on 3 x 5 flash cards, shuffle them and turn some so the definition is on top and others with the term facing up. You want a random set of cards in no specific order.

If it's an Art Appreciation class or similar, make three cards for each item you need to memorize. Paste or sketch the art object on one side and the artist on the back of the first card. Put the artist and the date on the second card, and the final card is the art object and date. You have separated all the combinations of facts you need to know, and you more efficiently learn and self-test your recall.

Start with three cards Select three cards at random from the full set of cards. Three cards represent six memorization tasks: three term-to-definition and three definition-to-term. This task is within normal short-term memory capability. Memorizing the terms will be quick and easy. The key is to shuffle the cards so they always appear in random order, mixing front and back each time you go through them. Then the term itself is the trigger, and not the order in which they appear.

Add cards one at a time When you have the first three cards firmly committed to memory, add one more card from the stack and repeat the shuffle, recite, shuffle, recite process until the fourth card is memorized. Note that you are reviewing three known terms while learning one new term and definition - not a memory overwhelming task.

When you have memorized the fourth card, add a fifth card from the stack and repeat the process until the new term is committed to memory. You want it to be at the over-learned level, or instant recall, not something you have to search your memory to produce.

No more than five cards at once Then, as you add additional cards one-at-a-time, drop one card already memorized so you never have more than five cards in the stack: four that you are reviewing, and one new term to learn.

When you have memorized the 25th card, add the previously memorized cards back, and review them twice with the shuffle and recite process. Put the cards aside and set a timer for 15 minutes to begin the spaced review process.

Long-term Memory

The task now is to put all the terms into long-term memory and change the slope of the forgetting curve. Research shows that without reviewing the terms, you will have forgotten 90% after 48 hours, with the greatest forgetting occurring in the first 20 minutes.

Spaced Reviews Systematic reviews will flatten the forgetting curve. Since research shows you lose nearly 40% within the first 20 minutes (and keep on losing without reviewing), the spaced intervals are important. Just set a timer, put the flashcards in your pocket, and go about your business. When you do frequent reviews, the time and effort to get back to 100% is minimal. Skip a review, and it will just take longer.

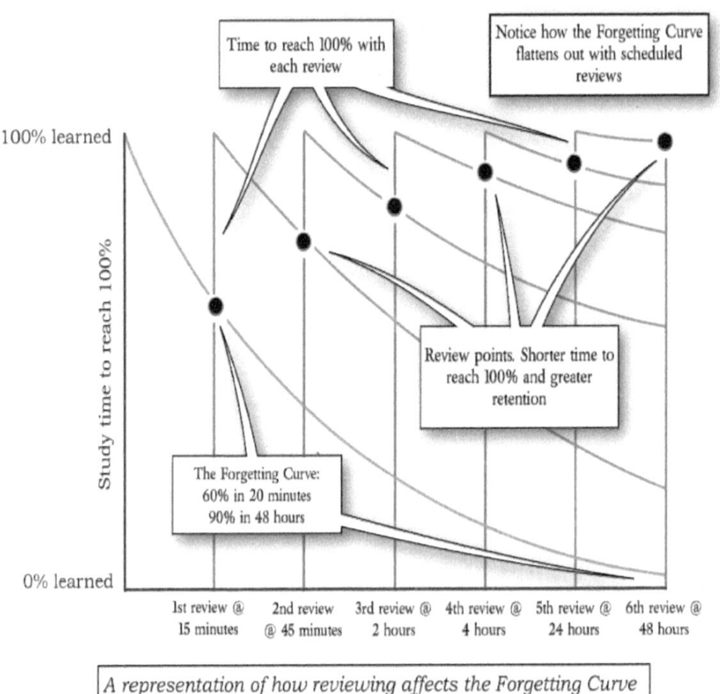

A representation of how reviewing affects the Forgetting Curve

The graph above shows the initial forgetting curve: an approximation of how fast you would forget without reviewing, and an illustration of the time it takes to reach 100% recall. Everyone forgets, but you want to flatten the shape of the curve with reviews, and you will decrease the time to get back to 100%.

Timed Review Is The Key Starting from when you reach 100% recall of the set of terms, the recommended system is to review 15 minutes later for the first review, then 30 minutes after that review. Then reviews expand to 2 hours later, and 3 hours after that. Finally, review your cards one time in each of the next two days.

For example, if you finish memorizing a list of terms and reached 100% recall at 1 p.m., you would do the first review at 1:15, then 2:00, followed by reviews at 5:00 and 7:00 that same evening. Continue with reviews around the same time for the next two days. Keep the stack of cards and go through them once a week.

Quick self-test When each interval is up, test your recall with the shuffle and recite process. When you come across a term you've forgotten (there won't be many), set it aside and spend a few minutes relearning those terms. Repeat at each interval.

This systematic review process is critical to solidifying the terms into long-term memory. Note that the longer you wait between reviews, the longer it will take to get back to 100%.

After this initial sequence, reviewing the terms weekly to monthly will keep them accessible. If you find that you struggle with recalling some terms, repeat the entire process with those difficult terms beginning with three, then four, then five in the shuffle and recite process. Review with the timed review process.

As you use new terms in your speaking and writing, you will move from memorization to embedded learning with the terms connected to each other and to other knowledge. (See Strategy 14: Vocabulary and Concept Mapping for an additional learning tool.)

STRATEGY 8

Do It Now !

Decide on a general topic

Gather hard facts about the topic on cards or pieces of paper

Record the source on each piece of paper

Sort and organize the facts

Draw a conclusion based on the facts

Turn the conclusion into a thesis statement

Write using the sorted and organized facts

Because

Starting with a general topic rather than a specific thesis statement gives more freedom to gather useful data. Recording facts and the source on individual cards makes it easy to sort and organize them. This also engages your mind in its natural effort to make sense of the set of facts. This makes it easy to draw a conclusion, which you then flip into a Thesis Statement.

> The writing comes easily, as you've done all the thinking before you begin.

A Simple Concept

Starting with a broad topic, find related, valid, and reliable resources, and identify significant facts. Sort those facts into categories related to the topic. After a Gestalt break, divide the facts within each category into pro- and con-groups, and organize them into an outline structure. Examine this full set of facts and draw a conclusion. Turn the fact-based conclusion into a thesis statement and write. As your research paper progresses, identify additional, specific facts needed to support your argument. This method allows you to quickly gather the needed facts.

Compare this to the amateur students' approach. The students are told to start with a thesis statement. With a lack of facts and no clue how difficult it will be to find information to support the thesis, they submit their thesis statement. Hoping to find what they need to write a coherent paper, they begin a frustrating search and frequently write a paper with insufficient resources.

This strategy reverses the process by starting with a set of credible facts that lead to a conclusion and a defendable thesis.

Thesis statement Create a thesis statement, if required, and confirm that the instructor will allow you to change the thesis statement as you begin your research and writing. Start with a topic you are interested in or curious about, but don't begin your research focused on this thesis.

Related sources of reliable information Gather a list of available and credible sources. Journals published in the subject area, authors with related expertise, and references in textbooks are good places to begin. Search the internet for "credible sources (topic area)," or "scholarly sources (topic area)," i.e., scholarly sources on poverty. Avoid news sites, Wikipedia, or ad-based sources. Always check with the librarian. They are a great resource for both local and online sources.

Thirty Articles or Books

Start with 30 pieces of scratch paper. On each piece of paper, write the full source's information — title, author, copyright, publisher, and page number. In the corner, write a code number to indicate the source (1, 2, 3, etc.). If you are in the library, take a handful of these sources to the copy machine. Skim the text, looking for a solid, quotable statement. Put the page on the copy machine with the scrap of paper showing the source detail in the corner and copy. You now have at least one related fact and the source for each page.

If you are online, create a folder titled with the source details. Be sure to get all the details needed to cite your source. When you find a quotable, factual statement, take a screenshot and save it to that source folder. Continue through the article or chapter, saving only pages with a solid factual statement.

Continue this process until you have at least 90 factual statements. Note that you are not trying to support any thesis or point of view, just collecting related facts.

Sorting The Facts

If you've taken screenshots of pages, print them out. Gather these, along with any copy machine pages. Go through them, identify the factual statements, and in the margin, write the code number related to the source. This is so you can always trace the individual quote back to the source. Then cut the factual statement(s) into individual pieces of paper in order to manipulate and sort them. You end up with at least 90 pieces of paper, each having a fact and the code for the source.

Randomize the 90+ pieces of paper. Throwing them all in the air works fine. Starting with your initial broad topic, e.g. Inner City, or whatever topic comes to mind after reading the individual fact, divide the facts into natural categories, such as:

- ◆ Inner city and CRIME
- ◆ Inner city and ECONOMICS
- ◆ Inner city and HOMELESS, etc.

Avoid having an "other" category. Label and paperclip each category. Set them aside. Take a short break.

Setting Up The Outline

Take one paper-clipped category at a time and divide the quotes into two sides of a coin. For example, the Inner City and CRIME might be divided into punishment and rehabilitation. ECONOMICS might be divided into the plight of the poor and suggested solutions. The categories should come from your mind and personal experience. Label each group and paperclip.

Take a longer break for your Gestalt mind to process this new outline of related facts. If possible, 24 to 48 hours is beneficial. During that time, as you do other activities, notice how often you have passing thoughts about the topic. That's your pre-conscious mind arranging and rearranging the information, and pre-writing your paper.

This next step needs some space, the floor or a large table. Unclip the bundles of quotes and lay them out in a large outline

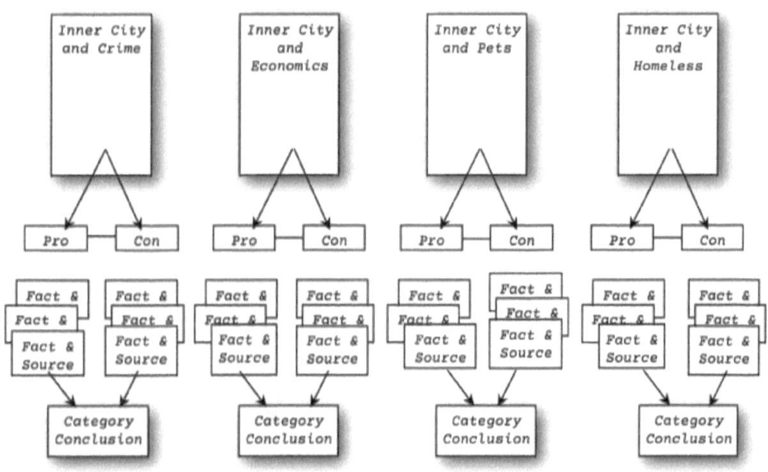

with the topic at the top, categories next, and the individual facts below. Then sit back and think about what conclusion you can draw from all of this. Listen to your pre-conscious mind!

Allowing time for the Gestalt to work is important. After you've arranged the set of facts on the table or floor, leave them and have a good night's sleep. When you wake up, look at the organized facts and listen to your brain. A conclusion/thesis will come easily.

Your Thesis

That conclusion becomes your thesis. If you see holes in the information, set out to gather the specific missing pieces of information. Since you know what you're looking for, it won't take long. Remember to record the sources so you can cite them in your paper.

The following graphic shows the process. Do the fact-gathering step in multiple stages to fit within your schedule. Remember, at this point you are not trying to gather evidence to support an idea—just gathering hard facts from which to draw a conclusion.

Your Gestalt mind works with all these facts. When it comes time to sort into categories, draw category conclusions, and the final overall conclusion, it comes easily, because you have both physically and mentally manipulated the facts.

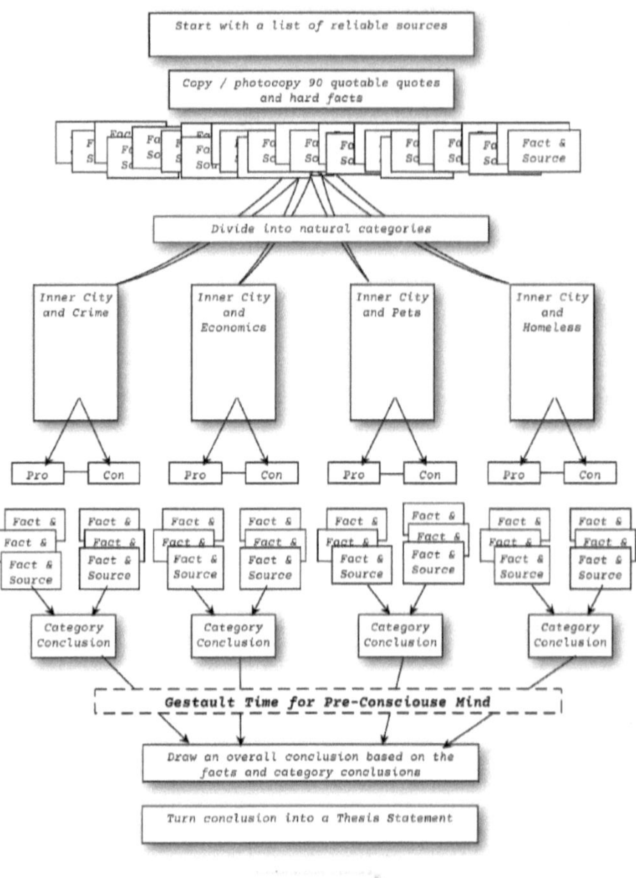

Start with a list of reliable sources
Copy / photocopy 90 quotable quotes and hard facts
Fact & Source
Divide into natural categories
Inner City and Crime
Inner City and Economics
Inner City and Pets
Inner City and Homeless
Pro
Con
Fact &
Fact &
Fact & Source
Category Conclusion
Gestault Time for Pre-Consciouse Mind
Draw an overall conclusion based on the facts and category conclusions
Turn conclusion into a Thesis Statement
WRITE !

Writing the paper flows easily, as you have already done all the thinking, and you have your facts in order. And if you sleep on it, when you awake, your pre-conscious mind has already finished nearly all the writing for you.

This strategy uses your pre-conscious mind and, while it is a different approach than the traditional prove-your-thesis approach, it's much easier and quicker to write a research paper. By gathering random facts and then manipulating them in a decision-making process, you actively engage your brain. Your brain is fully capable of taking the large number of related pieces of information and building connections and meaning between them.

STRATEGY 9

Do It Now !

Form a study group of no more than 5 people
Set rules about roles and tasks
Meet in person if possible
Rehearse presentations

Because

Groups of more than five may be difficult to schedule and may not be as efficient. Discussing tasks and responsibilities increases productivity. Live meetings are best where possible; conference calls or online meetings are functional. Rehearse group presentations to reveal problems with preparation, delivery strengths, and timing. Have a backup plan should a group member be unable to attend the presentation.

Study Groups

Studying with a few others is beneficial if everyone is committed, prepared, and dependable. Pick your study group members carefully and leave the group if others are not productive.

The best small group has three to five members, matching the three roles found in small groups: leader, taskmaster, and timekeeper. The leader organizes the study sessions, the taskmaster keeps group members on-task, and the timekeeper reminds everyone of deadlines and how much time is left in the session. These roles emerge naturally, but can be assigned.

Assigned Group Projects

An example: Four students are assigned to a group with the assignment to research and present a report on a topic. One student is diligent and dependable, one is a parent with two young children, one is a part-time student working two jobs, and the fourth member of the group is a party person more interested in the next fun activity. How can they organize to be successful?

Start by clarifying the task, what the instructor wants the group to accomplish, and the schedule for reaching the goal. Brainstorm solutions and tasks, where all contributions are accepted without judgment, followed by organizing and ranking them in terms of usefulness.

Break each task into small goals, and work in pairs to accomplish sub-goals. By focusing on small goals, differing schedules can be met and weaker students supported by partners. Regularly meet together as a group, in person, or electronically to assess progress.

As a group, outline the presentation and develop flashcards of the main points and important details. Divide the presentation into an introduction, body, and conclusion, with the weakest presenter doing the introduction, the strongest presenters doing the body, and all group members taking a small part in the conclusion. Practice at least twice while timing the presentation. Develop a backup plan should one of the group not make it to the presentation.

Supporting Learning In A Group

Studying need not be a solitary activity, and the act of explaining or defending a point of view enhances your own understanding and strengthens your learning.

Members of your study group can ask and answer questions to test and clarify understanding. In addition, meeting as a group with the instructor results in more complex answers that the study group can further discuss.

Your responsibility It's critical that you uphold your end of the group effort. Whatever your task, you must give it a high priority and produce a quality result on time. Meeting your responsibility with your best effort strengthens both your character and your reputation.

STRATEGY 10

Do It Now !

> When you have a question, first state two things that you know relate to the question, and then ask your question. When you understand the answer to your question, restate the answer in your own words.

Because

> By stating two things you know that lead up to your question, you provide the instructor with important clues to your problem. When you restate the answer in your own words, you will get further clarification from the instructor.

Stupid Question

How many times have you heard "There is no such thing as a stupid question?" Many, I'll bet, yet that's a ridiculous statement. Of course, there are stupid questions: questions completely off topic; questions just asked by another student and answered by the instructor; questions that make it clear that someone wasn't paying attention.

Don't Ask There are questions and statements that aren't exactly stupid, but don't give the instructor enough information to help you: "I don't get it. Could you repeat that?" Or "How can that be? I don't understand!" These questions, by themselves, don't give the instructor the details needed to provide a specific answer.

And even worse is asking a question in a way that offends the instructor. When a student says, "Huh? I don't get it," they are sending the message, "You are not a good teacher!" The instructor, being a normal human being, may go on the defensive: "I am a good teacher. You must be a poor student, either not paying attention or not very bright." Not the best basis for a student-teacher relationship when asking for help.

Two Plus One   There is a simple formula for asking questions that result in a better response, showing that you were paying attention, and also giving the instructor the clues to help clear up your confusion. And it's easy.

State two things that you know, then ask your question. That is, two statements related to what the instructor said, or was printed in the textbook, followed by your request for help.

Often, students think they understand point A, but they have it wrong. They don't realize it until it comes to point B, which doesn't follow what they erroneously thought point A was about. Then they ask the instructor to clarify point B, but that doesn't help. If you only ask about point B, the instructor has no way of knowing where your confusion originates. By including the two statements about what you know (or think you do), the instructor can zero in on the problem and clear up your confusion.

Example:

Student: "Earlier you said (point A)..... Just now, you said (point B).... How can that be?"

Instructor: "Ah, you misunderstood what I said earlier.... I said (clarified point A)...."

Student: "Got it! Now that makes sense."

This Strategy changes the message sent and received. By stating two things they know, the student sends the message "You are a good instructor and taught me two things. I am a good student, paying attention and engaged, but confused. Will you help me?"

Restate In Your Own Words

When you get an answer, and you now fully understand the issue, restate the answer in your own words. This identifies areas where you think you understand correctly, but actually you don't. The instructor can pinpoint the problem and provide additional help.

Use this strategy when asking in-class questions and when meeting in the instructor's office. This helps establish the basis for mutual respect and an ongoing positive relationship.

STRATEGY 11

Do It Now !

Sit up front in class.
Make eye contact with the instructor.
Provide visual feedback when you do, or don't,
understand.
Study in a quiet spot with minimal distractions.
Alternate input (reading, listening) and output
(notetaking, speaking aloud).

Because

Sitting at the front of the classroom will decrease
distractions and provide an opportunity to interact with
the instructor. Studying in a busy or noisy place with lots
of distractions makes it harder to concentrate. Also,
concentration is enhanced by changing the mode of
thinking from input to output and back to input. The
switch keeps your brain focused on the topic and reduces
the mental wandering.

Students study everywhere — dorm rooms or at home, cafeteria or McDonalds, library, or laying on the grass in the park. While it's good to take every opportunity to complete assignments, there are factors to consider in both where you sit in the classroom and where you study.

Where To Sit In Class

Where you sit in the classroom results in improved learning (and raises your grade) without you doing anything other than moving to the right spot. It's called the magic horseshoe. In a classroom of any size, the best grades will come from the front and center half-circle or horseshoe area, and the lower grades will come from the back rows. And it's not that the smart students all sit up front.

It has to do with distractions. If you sit as close to the front and center as you can, the instructor fills eighty percent of your view, and any movement on their part keeps your attention and focus on the subject. However, if you sit further back, everyone in front of you is a potential distraction. Every movement, every cough, every time someone turns to talk to the person next to them, distracts you. But front and center, with the instructor being eighty percent of your view, you are less likely to be drawn to those distractions.

Sit up front, pay attention, and learn more with no additional effort.

And there is one more advantage to sitting close to the instructor. You affect the pace of the lecture by giving visible feedback to the instructor. When you understand what the instructor is saying, give an affirmative nod. When you get confused, shake your head side-to-side. This movement attracts the instructor's attention, and the instructor repeats or re-explains what was unclear to you. If you sit in the back, they never notice your request for clarification.

Where To Study

I tracked students' time-on-task when studying in the school cafeteria. The worst case was when a student sat next to the aisle from the cafeteria entrance to the food line. He had the textbook open and was taking notes. When he prepared to leave, I asked him the purpose of his time in the cafeteria ("Studying") and how long he had been studying ("One hour"). Although he had been there for an hour, he had been on-task, reading or taking notes, for only twelve minutes!

The problem was distractions. Every time someone walked past him, he looked up. Every time someone laughed aloud, or dropped a fork, or scooted a chair, he looked up. These distractions broke his concentration and disrupted his learning. He would be the student who says, "I studied for an hour, but I can't remember anything I read."

Minimize Distractions The primary goal when studying is to minimize distractions. If you have to study in the cafeteria, sit in a corner facing away from others and distracting movements. If you study at home or in a dorm room, turn off the TV and your phone, and clear your desk of any clutter.

Do Not Disturb Put a sign on the door: "Studying! Do not disturb!" If you are between classes, find an empty classroom and spend your time reading and writing KEYWORD notes in the corner away from the door and windows.

Music Music can be a distraction or a tool for dealing with distractions. The brain pays attention to change — visual or auditory. Moving to an out-of-the-way location deals with the visual. Music can help cover sound distractions, but could also become its own distraction. The key is to have the same style of music, from rock to classical, playing without big changes. For example, an Apple or Amazon playlist of similar instrumental recordings blends into your mental background, as opposed to a pop music radio station with DJ comments and commercials. If you find yourself singing along, it's a distraction. Find another source or type of music.

Concentration A common concern among students is the inability to concentrate or to stay focused on the task at hand. Minimizing distractions is an efficient first step, and there are other strategies that improve concentration.

When dealing with new information, alternating input and output information keeps the brain engaged. Reading the textbook or watching a video are forms of input information going into your brain. If you do that for too long without a mental switch to output, your concentration fades and thoughts about something else intrude. However, if you alternate reading (input) with note-taking (output), as with the KEYWORD Notetaking, Notetaking Video, and Speed Read Novel strategies, you keep focused on the task. I designed these strategies to allow dividing a large task into smaller parts with breaks in between, which is another way to enhance concentration.

Your physical well-being also impacts concentration. A big meal or loads of sugar affects the oxygen going to your brain. Dehydration, whether from drinking too little water or too much alcohol the night before, significantly interferes with concentration, learning, and recall. Drugs, from cold medicine to cannabis, interfere with normal brain functioning. Your concentration suffers.

STRATEGY 12

Do It Now !

Control phone or computer interruptions to your study time.
Use only reliable sites in your research and writing.
Check your facts and look at opposing views
Don't take notes using a computer or tablet

Because

When you are focused and eliminate distractions, you are both more efficient and more effective in the use of your study time. Using only recognized and trustworthy sites ensures that you are dealing with the truth rather than just opinion. Regardless of the source, check your facts to confirm accuracy. Take notes in a paper notebook rather than electronically. You remember more when you make the transfer from screen to paper by handwriting your KEYWORD notes.

Distractions

Your biggest problem using a computer is being distracted by all the entertaining stuff - games, emails, Facebook - and the dings or beeps that alert you to the incoming whatever. Set the computer (and phone) to no interruptions and do NOT take a phone break in the midst of studying because you would spend more time on the computer or phone distractions than you planned.

The most necessary software is a word processor, and after that, an outlining or mind map program, a spreadsheet, and any websites that cover the content you are studying. Be sure whatever you use has a good spelling and grammar checker.

Who To Believe

The internet is full of untrustworthy sites. Start with the most reliable, such as sites ending in .gov or .edu. Also, check out:

- Google Scholar: https://scholar.google.com,
- Academia: Academia.edu,
- Directory of Open Access Journals: https://doaj.org

- Microsoft Academic:
  https://academic.microsoft.com/home
- Education Resources Information Center:
  https://eric.ed.gov
- For a list of others, see
  https://www.thoughtco.com/finding-trustworthy-sources-4114791

Fact Checking

There are also useful and reliable fact-checking websites. In today's atmosphere, it's important to verify claims, and look for opposing views. The International Society of Technology in Education (ISTE) has a list of the top ten fact checking sites: https://www.iste.org/explore/Digital-and-media-literacy/Top-10-sites-to-help-students-check-their-facts

Another site that has links to fact checking websites, and includes links from outside the USA is PRESSBOOKS, which has a Web Literacy for Student Fact Checkers site: https://webliteracy.pressbooks.com/chapter/fact-checking-sites/

Notetaking: Paper Is Better

I don't recommend taking notes on the computer, either before or during class. Research shows that notes taken by hand increase recall over electronic notes. The act of writing reinforces the ability to remember concepts and details. The exception to this is learning the vocabulary within a concept by using the computer to create a visual map of the vocabulary. (See Strategy 13: Vocabulary and Concept Mapping for more details and recommended software.)

If the material you are reading is on the internet, treat the screen like a textbook, and take KEYWORD notes in a notebook. Be sure to include the author and the URL of the website in your notes. Learn how to take screenshots of important graphs or illustrations, label them and save in folders with the course name.

STRATEGY 13

Do It Now !

Learn how to use the advanced features of a spell checker Always run your written work through a grammar and style checker.

Because

Spelling, grammar, and writing style checkers help fine tune your writing while teaching you to be a better writer. This avoids the instructor red marks and lower grades.

Spelling and grammar errors irritate instructors and can distract them from seeing what you are trying to say. As you progress through college, your thinking and writing becomes more complex, increasing the need for accurate spelling and correct grammar. Fortunately, technology exists that supports your efforts to write.

> While you can just use what your word processor
> provides, it is also worthwhile to make additional
> changes to raise the quality of your writing.

Spelling

Spell Checker   If correct spelling is a problem, or unfamiliar or technological terms are an issue, help is available. All word processors have a built-in spell checker. Set it to check while you type. Over time, the act of immediately identifying and correcting misspelled words improves your spelling.

Search Fields Type how you think a word is spelled in the search field of a browser, and a drop-down list of sites with options will pop up. You need to know how the word begins, but often the correct spelling will be found there.

Siri or Alexia Access Siri or Alexia and say the word. The response will be a correct spelling. You need to be quiet in certain settings and speak clearly.

Wild Card On certain sites, you can use a 'wildcard' in place of a missing letter, and it will provide all possible spelling options. For example, typing *place** will return *places, placed, and placing.* Wildcards are often used in searching research or library databases.

Grammar Checker

Word Processor Microsoft Word and most other major word processors include a grammar checker. By default, Word is set for a standard level of writing. Before you check your document, go to Tools, Spelling and Grammar, Options. Look for Writing Style and set it to Formal. This adds additional grammar rules appropriate for college-level writing.

Online Grammar Checker With an online grammar checker, copy and paste your text into an online website. Some have a free version, and some are a subscription. Don't bother with any version that does not include the option for an advanced level of writing. That is, some check grammar for general writing only, but others apply rules for academic or technical writing.

Commercial Grammar Checker Programs These are programs that stand alone, many with options to embed into a word processor. Grammarly, Premium Level, is a quality option and is a subscription service. There is an option to add Grammarly to Microsoft Word. Don't use the free version, as it is not robust enough for college papers. https://www.grammarly.com

Recommended   ProWritingAid is one option that incorporates more features than the word processor's built-in grammar checkers. You can use it both as an online paste-in-text option or as an add-on to both Windows and Macintosh programs. It has an extensive set of options and generates very useful reports about multiple aspects of your writing. It is a subscription service with a lifetime option and a 20% student discount.

ProWritingAid: https://prowritingaid.com

I recommend only the Premium Level. Download the free Premium version to test and be alert for additional discounts offered by the company.

STRATEGY 14

Do It Now !

Create a graphic map of the key words in a concept
Include both previously known and new words
Use the hide/show feature of outlining software

Because

A concept map strengthens your understanding of vocabulary much better than just dictionary definitions since it graphically shows the relationship of the terms to the main concept. When you include known words with new vocabulary, you connect the new knowledge to previous knowledge, increasing recall. The hide/show software feature tests your ability to recall the entire concept, starting with only a single clue.

Vocabulary Is Key To Thinking

Typically, when students think of vocabulary, it's related to the glossary at the end of the book or an assignment to memorize a list of important terms. Those lists are most often in alphabetical order, suitable for a dictionary. And yes, you can use the Memorization Strategy to learn a list of terms and definitions quickly, but there is another way to enlarge your vocabulary.

Expanding your vocabulary in a specific subject area is an important step in being able to think, talk, and write about a concept in that area. Without the core vocabulary, you won't be able to understand advanced concepts. Instead of memorizing a list, you can use the terms to develop a deeper understanding through concept mapping.

Concept Mapping

Concept mapping is a graphic technique to display the relationship between terms related to a central topic. In developing a concept map, you create a structure of knowledge about that topic, integrating new terms into your existing knowledge.

A list of terms, alphabetized or not, does nothing by itself to aid in learning the terms. The visual structure of a concept map accesses a different part of your brain and makes recall easier. When you take a list of terms and create a visual map, you identify the relationships between the terms as well as manipulate them.

Here is a sample of a simple vocabulary list related to Ecosystems:

◆ Bacteria

◆ Biotic Factors

◆ Carnivore

◆ Consumer

◆ Decomposer

◆ Ecosystems

◆ Herbivore

◆ Omnivore

◆ Organism

◆ Plants

◆ Producer

These are important terms, but it's just a list. Below, the concept map of Ecosystems provides a graphic of the terms and how they are interrelated. Even without knowing the meaning of the terms, you can gain insight into how they relate to the main topic.

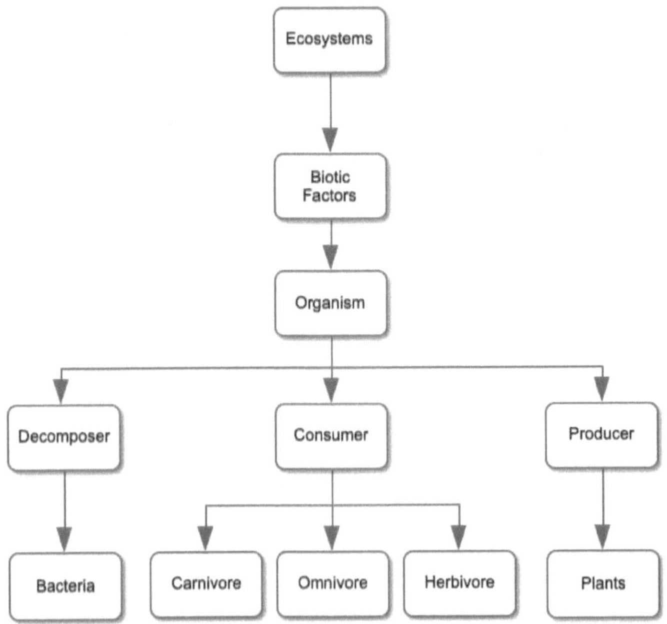

Use a Computer You will make deep learning easier when you use a computer, and the software mentioned in *Strategy 7: Memorization* and *Strategy 12: Using a Computer*, to build your concept map. Then, using the hide and show feature of the program, collapse the concept map down to the main topic. Test your recall by seeing if you can remember the next level of headings, and review by applying the hide/show feature. Now move to one of the subheadings and apply the hide and show feature again.

Repeat for all the subheadings. When finished, draw the complete map of terms and their relationships just from looking at the main term, proving that you have the concept firmly in your memory.

Study the concept map on the previous page and imagine a blank concept map. On the next page, do a self-test. Notice how useful the visual graphic is in aiding recall.

Look at the heading Organism. Can you recall the three items connected to that heading?

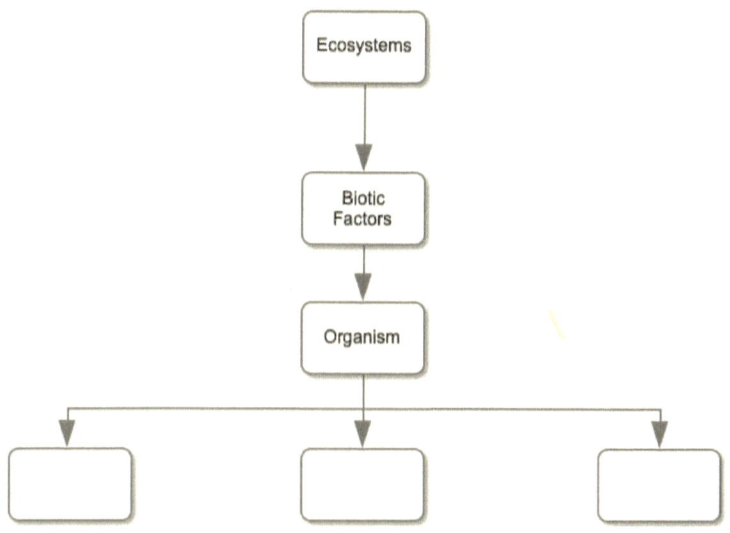

Then look at the next row of headings. Can you recall the terms below them?

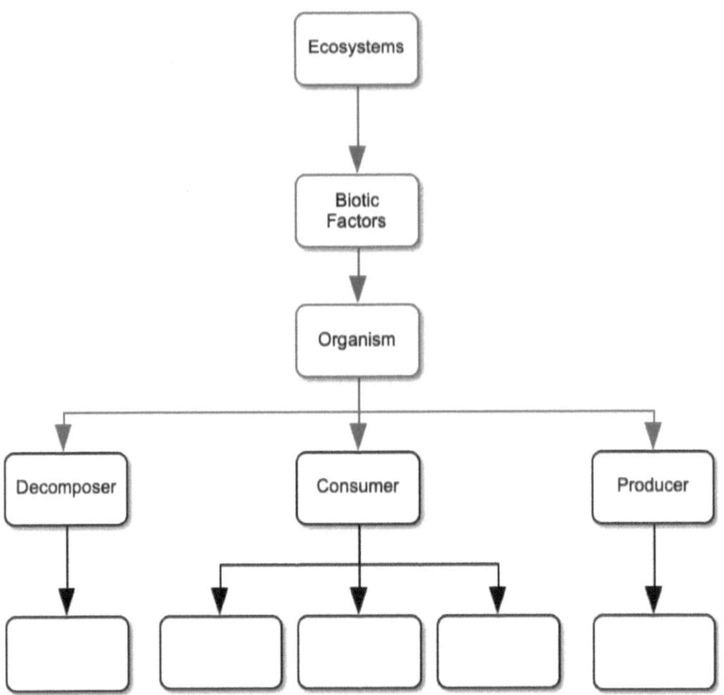

Even without a computer, use the hide and show technique by covering the boxes with a card to test your recall. Replicate the concept map from the initial heading by mentally creating each additional level.

To apply this strategy to an assigned vocabulary, draw a concept map using both the terms in the assigned list and any additional terms needed to complete the concept. When you include additional terms that you already know are related to the concept, you connect this new knowledge to your prior knowledge - a powerful aid to recall.

STRATEGY 15

Do It Now !

Review KEYWORD notes and flash cards
Go through the test, answering only those items where
you have instant recall
Go through the test again, answering items where you
recognize the correct answer after looking at the choices
Go through the test again, eliminating choices you know
are incorrect, and pick an answer at random (guess).
Go through the test one last time, looking for items you
may have missed answering.
Do NOT change an answer once you have marked it.

Because

Reviewing your notes brings the details into your
conscious mind because the abbreviated notes cause you
to practice recall based on minimal clues.

Starting with answering the items you are absolutely sure of packs correct answers to the beginning of the test period and builds your most accurate recall paths.

The second time through the test is a recognition level recall and builds on the first time through.

What's left are items where you don't solidly know and don't recognize — the guess level. Eliminate items you can tell are incorrect and select an answer from what remains. Don't change an answer, as you are more likely to change from correct to wrong.

Review KEYWORD Notes

Multiple-Choice test taking is primarily a matter of recall of stored information. The best preparation is to review your KEYWORD notes and any flash cards you have used to memorize a set of terms, dates, etc. This is best done the evening before the test, avoiding last-minute cramming.

Amateur Mistakes

This strategy is about how to take a test and avoid making recall less effective. First, let's look at what happens when amateurs take a multiple-choice test. They study by rereading the chapter and/or their notes at the last minute. Having no strategy to confirm knowing the content, they begin the test with the nervous thought, "I hope I know this stuff." They start with item one and proceed item by item through the test, and often run out of time before finishing.

The problem with this approach is what happens within the brain as you search through stored links between facts, trying to recall a specific answer. When you choose an incorrect answer, you have followed or created an incorrect path for that test item, which increases the likelihood of retracing that incorrect path on another test item.

Example: The test question asks the amateur to pick the vice-president for the fourth President of the United States. If you think James Monroe was the fourth president instead of James Madison, you will pick Daniel Tompkins as vice-president. Then, any other test items related to the fourth president, such as dates served, wars fought, laws passed, increase the likelihood of choosing an incorrect answer.

Taking The Test With A Plan

The Multiple-Choice Test Taking Strategy does the opposite, strengthening recall paths to correct information, and the test items you are not sure of have an increased chance of being answered correctly.

Multiple-choice test items are made up of a stem (the question) and multiple foils (potential answers). Reading the stem starts your brain searching for related information. The strategy uses how the brain functions to answer more items correctly.

Step One - Instant Recall   Read the stem for the first question, and if you can complete it <u>without reading the foils</u>, you will have traced the path to your strongest chance of a correct answer. Then look at the foils to see if what you thought is one of the choices. If so, mark it. If it's not among the choices, don't answer this test item at this time. Go through the entire test, reading the stems and only answering those where you know the answer without looking at the foils. If you read a stem and can't immediately provide the answer, skip that question. Don't even stop to look at the foils.

In this step, you create two advantages: strengthening your recall for those items where your knowledge is strongest, the 2 + 2 = 4 or instant recall level, and packing all of your most likely correct answers at the beginning of the test period.

Step Two - Recognition Go back to the beginning of the test to the first unanswered item. Read the stem and all the foils carefully. When one of the foils jumps out as the right answer, mark it, and move to the next item. If you are not sure which foil is the correct response, don't complete that item; skip it. You are answering only those test questions you are positive are correct once you see the choices.

In this step, you build off of the most likely correct responses in Step One, and answer those items that you instantly recognize as correct once you see the choices. This is your second strongest set of responses.

Step Three - Eliminate and Guess Again, return to the beginning of the test and the first unanswered item. Read the stem and foils, but reverse the process and look for foils that are obviously incorrect. Eliminate those foils and randomly select one of the remaining foils. These are the items that are not instant recognition, nor where the answer is obvious once the choices are viewed. Your best option is to eliminate answers you know to be wrong and guess among the remaining choices.

Step Four - Check for missing answers Since you have skipped items in the first two steps, there is a chance you have not answered a question. Go through the items one by one and confirm that you have answered each one.

Do NOT change a previous answer, as you more often change from correct to wrong. With this strategy, you have packed the highest percentage of correct answers into the beginning of the timed test (all tests are timed tests) and left guessing to the very end. If you run out of time, you lose only the weakest answers.

STRATEGY 16

Just Do It !

Review your notes

Create 3 questions you think will be on the test, and take a break

Create 3 more questions that will be on the test, and take a break

Create a final 3 questions that will be on the test, and take a break

Randomly select 3 questions, set a timer for 10 minutes, and outline your answers.

Repeat selecting sets of 3 questions and outlining answers within 10 minutes for each set.

When taking the test, first outline all the questions, then select your best outlines to begin writing your answers.

Because

When you create questions, you are using everything you've learned in the text and lecture to determine what the instructor values and will include on the test. You are exercising the thinking required in an essay test and not just recalling facts.

The short breaks allow your pre-conscious mind to process the questions and form responses. By outlining the practice questions under time pressure, you practice the exact thinking you need when taking the test.

When outlining the actual test questions before starting to write, you bring your knowledge to the conscious level, facilitate recall, and generate your best answers at the beginning of the test.

Using The Correct Brain Parts

Essay is NOT Multiple Choice We've all taken both multiple-choice and essay tests, and it's obvious that there is a great difference between them. Each type of test accesses a different part of your brain - one looking for recognition and recall of facts, and the other asking you to combine ideas and concepts to show cause and effect or other relationships between the facts. Therefore, studying for an essay test should differ significantly from studying for a multiple-choice test. This strategy shows you how to do that.

The right kind of practice There are two parts to this strategy: test preparation and test taking. In preparation for the test, you exercise the part of your brain needed to answer essay questions by creating potential test questions.

Think like the instructor What is the instructor most passionate about? What did they emphasize most strongly in the lecture? What in your in-class notes goes beyond what the textbook presents? All these are clues to what the essay test will include. Here is a useful resource - a guide for instructors on how to write essay questions:

https://testing.byu.edu/handbooks/WritingEffectiveEssay Questions.pdf

Before you begin to practice, you want to know some basic things: How many questions will be on the exam? What topics will the test cover? How much time will you have to complete the test?

Gather your notes and any old quizzes or tests from this instructor. This is a good time to study with two or three friends who have gone to class, paid attention, and taken notes. The goal is to solidify your knowledge together, not to teach those who've not paid attention in class.

Step One: The Easy Level Whether you are studying by yourself or with friends, the first step is to review your notes. Translate your KEYWORD notes and carefully read your in-class notes to bring all that knowledge to the surface. With your friends, or by yourself, think and talk about the instructor's values and beliefs, and try to determine what could be most important to the instructor - important enough to be included in the essay exam.

Create the test Now, make up three questions you think the instructor will include on the test. The more you discuss or argue about the questions, the better they will be. This is an active mental task, and you are deeply processing everything you've learned from this class, the textbook, and elsewhere. Write the questions on 3-by-5 cards and set them aside.

Take a break. Your mind works through the questions you've created and brings any stored information you have to bear at the pre-conscious level. This is an example of how the Gestalt works: As you take a break, walk across campus, get some refreshments, or talk about totally unrelated topics, your preconscious mind is actively working on answering the questions you created, and you couldn't stop it if you wanted. You set up a puzzle in your mind, and it has to work at resolving that puzzle.

Step Two: Digging deeper Make up an entirely different test with three questions that you firmly believe the instructor could include on the test. This second round requires you to mentally dig even deeper into the content and into the instructor's values. You are actively thinking and discussing the possible questions, and this activates your mind productively.

Take another break. These breaks can be from 10 minutes to a full day. During the break, your preconscious mind mulls over everything in a powerful process of consolidating your learning.

Step Three: Complex Thinking Then, one last time, create three new questions that you predict will be on the test. Again, your mind is engaged with everything you know about the subject - even beyond what is in the text or presented in the lecture. This is the exact thinking you do when you answer essay questions.

Practice Thinking Under Pressure

Shuffle all the cards and put them face down on the table. Set a timer for 10 minutes and randomly pull three cards from the pile. Outline your answer to all three questions within the 10 minutes, including as much detail in the outline as you would need to answer the question fully. You need not write out the answer.

Then reset the timer, select three new questions, and repeat the process. Keep doing this until you've gone through all the questions.

Realize that you have exercised your brain doing the exact task that the essay test will require of you. Rather than just rehearsing facts and reviewing notes, you have set your mind to answer more complex questions in a limited amount of time.

The Professional Edge

To take the professional edge, there is one more step. Make an appointment with the instructor, either as an individual or as a group, and explain that you are preparing for the test by making up and answering questions. Assure the instructor you are not trying to find out what actual questions will be on the test, but only if the questions you created are good questions, in an appropriate style and level of complexity.

Answer one question Before you go to the instructor with the questions, pick, individually or as a group, the strongest single question, the one most likely to be on the test. Write out your answer to the question completely. Give it to the instructor and ask, "If this were a question on the test, is this the kind of answer you are looking for?"

The feedback you get in this process is invaluable in understanding what instructors value both as a question and the type of answer they expect. You're getting the feedback that would appear on your paper when it's handed back, but you're getting it before the test. And don't be surprised to find some of your questions, whole or in part, appearing on the actual test. Remember, your mind continues to process the questions, your answers, and the feedback from your instructor at the pre-conscious level - bringing together all of your mental power to prepare for the exam.

The Big Day

Reviewing combined notes You have both the pre-class notes taken from the textbook and the aligned in-class notes. Translate your KEYWORD notes into full thoughts, and carefully review the added information presented in class. Do this within 24 hours before the test to bring everything to the surface of your conscious mind. You realize that you are better prepared than you have ever been. Take a deep breath - and begin.

Outline before you write Look at each essay question, and on scrap paper or in the margin, create an outline of your answer. Do this for all the questions before you start to write. Two reasons for this: one, your outlines are more complete and accurate at this stage, rather than after you have answered a specific question; two, you may find that the question you would have answered first isn't your best beginning, and you know this as you create the outlines. If you run out of time, do it on questions where your recall is sketchy.

A scenario: amateur students look over the questions and spot one they feel confident about answering, and immediately start writing. As they get into the middle of their answer, they find they can't remember a significant point. They then spend time trying to recall that point, and their stress level goes up (which interferes with recall), and they cannot get to the last couple of questions.

But you, the professional student, go through each question and do an outline of the main points for each. More and more facts and talking points come into your consciousness, which lessens your stress about the entire test. You select the question that has the most complete outline, quickly work through your answer, and move on to the next best question. Because the outlines bring information into your mind easily, you finish the test in time to review your answers and make minor corrections or additions. In the end, you know you have done well on the test.

Follow Up   As soon as possible after the test, take two minutes to make notes about the types of questions asked on the test. Were they asking for a cause-and-effect answer, compare and contrast, or an evaluation of a concept? How close were your created questions to what was on the test? This helps you to be better prepared for the next test.

Build your essay test-taking skills   When you get the test back from the instructor, don't just look at the grade and move on. Take the time to improve your essay writing skills. Select the question and answer that you could improve the most. Using any feedback on the returned test, or your better answers to other questions as a guide, rewrite your answer completely.

Meet with the instructor and take both the original and your rewritten answer. Tell them you are not asking to change your grade, but you'd like to improve your ability to answer essay questions. Ask if the rewritten version would have been a better answer. You will get the personal and invaluable feedback that strengthens your ability to do even better on any essay exam.

PARTING ADVICE

- **Never skip a class.** Ever. If it's a real emergency or you are deathly ill, give the instructor some form of verification. If you skip the first class, it will be easier to skip the next class. Don't even start.

- **Never be late for a class.** See above. When you come in late, you'll be noticed by the instructor in a negative way.

- **Talk to the instructor.** Give a compliment. Ask a question. Disagree with an idea. And listen. Say Thank You.

- **Alcohol and weed dehydrate you** and your brain needs a massive amount of water to function well. Don't drink the night before an exam. Or do drugs. It will not turn out well.

◆ **The purpose of college** is to challenge your current knowledge and beliefs. When a concept seems confusing or is counter to what you already know, consider it carefully. This is growth taking place.

◆ **Put a 'Do Not Disturb' sign** on your door and be blunt to those who interrupt. Tell others you are studying and will be available later. Turn off your phone.

◆ **If you really want a boost** in your recall, review your KEYWORD notes or flashcards right before you go to bed. Your mind continues to consolidate your learning while you sleep.

◆ **Find places to study** that are quiet and convenient. Use every spare minute to apply these strategies, most of which are designed to be easily divided into smaller steps.

◆ **Don't believe everything you read,** or are told. Think, disagree, argue—and listen with an open mind. That's the lifelong process of being an engaged, educated person.

◆ **Intend to learn,** to be successful, to be committed, to do your best! Intent is the driving force behind becoming successful at anything.

◆ **Focus on learning** and the grades will follow. When you have the knowledge, the rest is easy.

◆ **And about AI.** Cheat, and you will fail, if not now, in the future when you have to think for yourself.

John L. Tenny, Ph.D.
learningpathpress@gmail.com

These strategies were not created by a straight-A student.
They were discovered by someone who was failing—

until one moment changed everything.

The story behind the Sixteen Study Strategies

Author and Study Resources

Visit John's Author page,
teaching resources, and study tools.

————————————————————

Send John a note—*he reads every message.*

LearningPathPress@gmail.com
Author ° Speaker ° Study Tools

————————————————————

When the First A Changed My Life

*"John's memoir that tells the story of his
academic struggles and his path to
learning how he learns."*